DATE DUE

Demco

RAILROADS OF THE WEST

This is the world's last Kitson Meyer steam locomotive, built in the early 20th century. The steam train has been outmoded by new technology, including magnetic levitation, for a faster, smoother ride.

RAILROADS OF THE WEST

HANNAH STRAUSS MAGRAM

MASON CREST PUBLISHERS

Mason Crest Publishers
370 Reed Road
Broomall PA 19008

First printing

1 3 5 7 9 8 6 4 2

Library of Congress Cataloging-in-Publication Data
on file at the Library of Congress

ISBN 1-59084-073-9

Publisher's note: many of the quotations in this book come from
original sources, and contain the spelling and grammatical
inconsistencies of the original text.

CONTENTS

Chinese and Filipino workers lay track for the Great Northern Railroad in Washington State. Chinese railroad workers were known for their hearty work ethic, a trait that increased the efficiency of railroad construction throughout the west during the 19th century.

BLASTING A ROAD OF RAILS

IN THE AUTUMN OF 1868, A CREW OF CHINESE-
AMERICAN RAILROAD WORKERS STOOD ATOP A
2,000-foot cliff in California, dangling a 15-year-old boy over
the side. Suspended by 500-foot-long ropes and swaying in icy
wind, the boy labored with a pickaxe. He drilled small holes
into the granite rock around him. At last, he signaled to the
men above to send down their most important tool: dynamite.

Stuffing the dynamite into each hole, the boy lit a fuse and
quickly jerked on the rope to signal "explosion!" A moment's
delay could mean instant death. As the boy jerked himself back
up the rope, the dynamite sent out a blast of rocky chunks.

Day after day, the workers sparked explosions to carve
out ledges and tunnels in the mountains. They **toiled**
endlessly to clear a path for America's incredible new road—
a "road made of rails."

In America's western states, many of the men working on
the railroads could understand only a few words of the English
language. When California railroad companies needed workers,
they had advertised in newspapers in southern China. More
than 14,000 Chinese workmen applied for railroad jobs. They

West of the Mississippi River in the 1860s, the new railroads were the first roads across much of America. Railroad surveyors had to travel through lonely areas to search for good routes. In the forests, railroad crewmen rarely saw the lights of towns. Clearing a track was hard work: the men had to chop trees, blast the tree stumps, shove huge boulders out of the way, and level the rocky ground. Clearing a path through one mile of woods could be 10 days of hard work for 300 men.

left their homes and sailed for two months across the Pacific Ocean. These Chinese immigrants came to dig tunnels, build railroad **trestles**, and lay miles of track across the American West.

In 1866, there were only 6,000 Chinese workers, but by 1867 nearly 50,000 Chinese were living in the state of California. These immigrants arrived with knowledge of how to irrigate river valleys for farming. By 1872, two-thirds of vegetables grown in the soil of California were Chinese farmers' crops.

Western companies had first tried to hire local California miners rather than immigrants. But **Gold Rush** fever was in the air: thousands of American workers were distracted by the excitement of gambling. Men wanted to look for gold and "strike it rich" in Nevada. Although many Americans signed up to work on the railroads, most soon quit to go search for gold mines.

Chinese workmen, however, were willing to **persevere** in the rugged railroad labor. They worked from dawn till dusk, six days a week. Cholera, explosives accidents, and harsh weather

Alfred Nobel invented commercial dynamite at his family's factory in St. Petersburg in 1866. Dynamite was safer and easier to use than nitroglycerine, a highly explosive liquid. When Alfred Nobel began to market dynamite in the late 1860s, American railroad crews were able to use the explosive to move mountains.

killed nearly 2,000 Chinese workers, but more Chinese came to take their places in the work crews. By summer 1868, 90 percent of railroad crewmen working in California's Sierra Nevada Mountains were Chinese.

Travelers returned from California with the amazing story.

4/3 SNOW SHED, ALPINE PASS

In order to keep rail layers productive through the winter, snow sheds were built over the rails. These shelters protected the rail lines from harsh weather conditions, allowing the trains to continue running.

They described Chinese workers suspended from cliffs. The workers stood in hanging bosun's chairs, which were sturdy hand-made canvas baskets of the type that sailors use over the side of ships. Modern work crews still lower baskets and scaffolding down the sides of tall buildings and bridges to hold workmen.

The American wilderness proved to be beautiful but harsh for everyone. In winter, workers sometimes had to dig through

18 feet of snow to reach the ground and lay tracks. In 1866, harsh blizzards dumped 44 feet of snow on the weary crews. A sudden **avalanche** could bury men alive.

"Shoveling, wheeling, carting, drilling, blasting rocks and earth," wrote one man in his journal in 1865. He was describing the hard work of blasting railroad tunnels. Work was usually slow and **tedious**. Sometimes the workers could drill only a few inches of granite in an entire day. Moving all of the equipment was an enormous job; the crew needed fresh rails, ties, spikes, and rods every step of the way. Each iron rail weighed 700 pounds; it took five railroad men to carry one rail and lift it into place.

This iron road would be strong enough to bear the weight of a nation. When the clanging of iron began to sound in the American West, the steel of American cities soon arrived.

The distance between the rails (called the gauge) on tracks in the United States is 4 feet, 8.5 inches. This gauge was used because it was the same gauge railroads in England used. But where did the distance come from?

The spacing was used because because the first people who built railroads and railroad cars used the same tools which were used to build wagons, and wagons used that wheel spacing. The wagons had to keep that amount of space between their wheels, because the wheels had to fit the deep ruts in the old dirt roads. The roads date back to the first century A.D., when they were built by Roman soldiers. So the specifications for railroads in America were determined by the width of Roman war chariots built more than 2,000 years ago.

👆 This is an early print of the Rocket, a locomotive built by George Stephenson. Although the locomotive was just a curiosity at first, excitement about the railroad soon caught on across the country.

2

HARNESSING THE POWER OF STEAM

SINCE THE BEGINNING OF TIME, HORSES HAD BEEN THE FASTEST TRANSPORTATION FOR humans traveling on dry land. At the end of the 18th century, suddenly this changed forever. A few brilliant individuals in England and the United States thought of using steam to power land transportation. An English inventor built the first steam-powered **locomotive**. One American inventor wrote that he could picture "the time [in the future] when carriages propelled by steam will be in general use, traveling at the rate of fifteen to twenty miles an hour…as fast as birds can fly."

In England's cold, rainy climate, people burned coal in order to heat their homes and their buildings. Coal miners dug sooty coal out of the ground and dragged it in heavy loads to every fireplace, in every corner of the country. In 1781, a coal miner's son named George Stephenson designed a way to ease the burden: he invented a steam-powered "traveling machine" that could help to haul coal.

During the mid-1800s, enthusiastic businessmen competed to improve trains. In 1851, refrigerator cars were the newest luxury on the railroad. For the first time, farmers could safely transport perishable foods. Railroads could carry products like butter to customers all over the country. The Pullman sleeping car was another new luxury. Passengers could sleep in bunk beds during long overnight trips on the railroads. Pullman's sleeper cars had cushioned seats that converted into beds, and upper beds folded out of the walls above. George Pullman also designed dining cars. Decades before the year 2000, luxury American trains would offer heat, air conditioning, bathrooms, electrical outlets, and telephones.

Stephenson, an uneducated man who never learned to read, was able to interest people in the **utility** of his new locomotive. His steam-driven Rocket could pull a train of carts faster than horses could pull a carriage. In 1823, Stephenson and his son Robert designed a track made of iron. Two years later, traveling at the speed of eight miles per hour, a steam engine pulled the world's first passenger railcar on the Stephensons' iron track.

Peter Cooper, a New Yorker with only a year of schooling, manufactured the first American-built steam locomotive to run on a chartered American railroad. In Baltimore, Maryland, Cooper founded the Canton Iron Works. He built a small steam engine, the Tom Thumb, that successfully steamed along a track. Steam engines were becoming famous on both sides of the Atlantic Ocean. By 1829, a British train could reach the speed of 35 miles per hour for the first time in history.

The new idea of steam power seemed less attractive to stagecoach drivers, **turnpike** companies that built toll roads, and captains of canal barges. These men felt anger toward the new railroad vehicles that would be able to transport people and supplies so rapidly on land. They feared that railroads would put their stagecoaches and canal barges out of business.

The Erie Canal, built in 1825, was America's most famous "water road." It transported live animals, people, food, clothing, and supplies. A canal is an artificial waterway, and the Erie Canal was built to connect the Hudson River, in New York on the east coast, to people living in the Great Lakes region and the Midwest. It offered Americans an easy, inexpensive water route. The years of the "Canal **Boom**" were a time for people to travel and trade on America's rivers.

But huge areas of America do not have river routes. In the 1850s, railroad tracks began to offer land roads into the prairie states. Thousands of settlers arrived by train. In the middle of the continent, in Illinois and nearby states, farmers came to grow wheat and corn. Railroads and canals were competing furiously for all the new passengers and **commerce**.

Peter Cooper built the first American steam locomotive, the Tom Thumb. In 1830, his engine lost a race with a horse-drawn car on the tracks of the Baltimore and Ohio Railroad. Soon, however, steam engines would achieve speeds that horses could not match.

Canal barge captains tried to spread rumors and false advertising. They wanted to convince people that riding a "dangerously fast" 30-miles-per-hour train would rattle passengers' brains. The new railroads, like many new inventions in history, faced fierce opposition from all the workers and businesses it replaced.

Bad publicity does not fool people for long; Americans liked the idea of a rail track. Lines of track were helping horses glide heavy loads across short distances. America's first railroad, the Baltimore & Ohio line, was already using horses to pull carriages along a track in 1830. But what about longer distances of track, across hundreds and hundreds of miles?

An inventor named John Stevens insisted that it would be possible to lay a long-distance track. At first, no one believed him. The idea sounded wild. Gradually, John Stevens's idea captured the imagination of some Americans. Businessmen wanted longer sections of track for horse-drawn carts; some men experimented with attaching wind sails to the carts; others tried running a horse on a treadmill inside a cart. But steam-powered engines, racing from one city to another? This idea still sounded like science fiction. Finally, excitement began to spread: in 1829, operators imported a British locomotive to the United States.

One year later, the first American steam passenger train came chugging out of Charleston in South Carolina. This changed the idea of "people in motion." Soon, the clatter of iron and steel, and the sound of railroad whistles grew louder than the voices of the past.

More and more Americans realized that the railroad could be a **conduit** of commerce and luxury. In the eastern part of the United States, businessmen and government officials rushed to **charter** rail lines. They knew this would promote trade between towns and cities. Like the **arteries** that spread life through a human body, railroad lines began to spread life throughout the nation. By 1860, America had more than 30,000 miles of track on the ground in states in the East.

America's Civil War began in 1861. The huge armies of the North and the South needed men and supplies. For the first time in history, armies used railroads in war. In 1862, the Northern army formed the United States Military Railway, with military and hospital trains marked USMR on the sides of the cars. Railroad supply routes were extremely important to both sides. The North and the South each targeted their enemy's railroad tracks. Many battles took place along tracks in Tennessee, Georgia, and other states. Raiders used weapons and explosives to derail trains and blow up railroad bridges.

In the famous Andrews Raid, Northern raiders stole a Southern locomotive and began racing it northward toward the town of Chattanooga. Southern trainmen chased after them by driving another locomotive at full speed in reverse. The raiders damaged wires and equipment until the locomotive finally rolled to a halt. Southern trainmen captured and hanged most of the Northern raiders. The wild

A man drives two mules pulling a tourist barge up the Erie Canal. At one time barges like this would be full of goods being shipped to other parts of the country.

event became known as the Great Locomotive Chase.

The Northern army, known as the Union Army, had longer rail routes than the Southern Confederate Army. Northern army and navy soldier were able to attack Southern rail lines.

The first "transcontinental" railroad was built across the isthmus of Panama, a narrow strip of land that connects North America with South America. People traveling west from New York would sail to Panama's east coast, travel by train to the Pacific coast, then take a ship north to California. Today the Panama Canal cuts through this land, allowing ships to pass from the Atlantic into the Pacific Ocean.

The Northern victory over the South was due to the Union's superior railroad: when General Sherman marched to capture Atlanta in the South, the railroad supplied his troops for 200 days. Every day, 16 trains each carried 200,000 pounds of ammunition, food, and medical supplies to the Union Army.

The Civil War ended in 1865. Thousands of soldiers left military life to look for employment. Strong young men signed up to work on the western railroads. By the early 1900s, railroads would employ more Americans than any other industry in the country. Approximately one of every 50 citizens worked for the railroads.

The year 1865 also was an important one for the steel industry. Before the Civil War, America was not producing enough iron to supply the railroads. Companies had to import iron from across the Atlantic Ocean. American railroad tracks were made of used rails from England; importers re-rolled the worn-out British rails before using them to lay new American tracks. In the 1860s, a brilliant Scottish American became the leading steel manufacturer. His name was Andrew Carnegie. His skillful management helped transform the steel and railroad business: by 1890, America was producing three times as much iron a day. Manufacturers began to use a new process for rolling red-hot steel in American steel mills. In the steel mills of Pittsburgh and Chicago, iron and carbon would now transform into steel at a pace that was faster than ever in history.

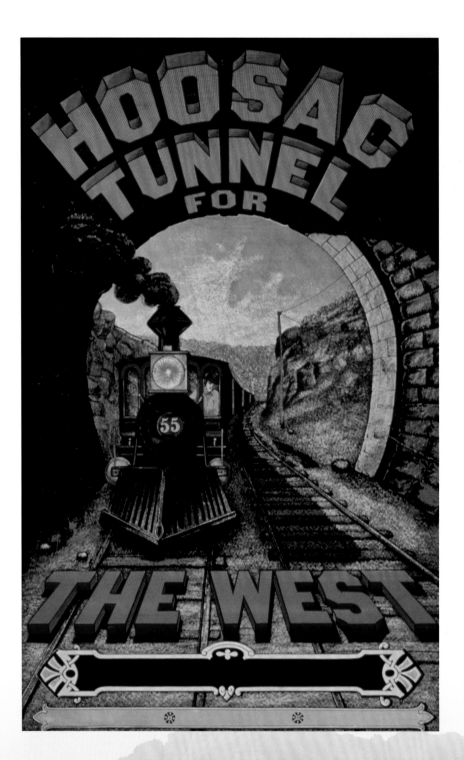

BUILDING TRACKS IN THE WEST

BRILLIANT ENGINEERS FELT THEY COULD
EXTEND RAILROAD TRACKS TO THE WESTERN
states. One of these daring men was Theodore D. Judah. He
knew the difficulty of traveling across the United States. Judah
had journeyed to California: the trip took months. Judah sailed
south along the Atlantic Ocean coast to Central America, rode
stagecoaches for weeks to reach the Pacific Ocean coast of
California, sailed up the coast, then finally came ashore to
travel in several more stagecoaches to reach the town of
Sacramento. Judah knew that Americans could use the
convenience of a nation-wide railroad.

> 🐦 This poster promoted one of the western
> railroads in the mid-19th century. It was not hard
> to convince people that railroad travel was the best
> way to go west—it was cheaper, faster, and safer
> than traveling in a wagon train across the country.

Leland Stanford (1824–1893) was a lawyer and grocery store owner. He came to California during the Gold Rush. His knowledge of the law helped him settle arguments between the miners. Stanford ran for state treasurer in 1857. He lost the race but found that he liked being in politics. He ran for governor in 1859 and lost, but was elected governor of California in 1861 and served a two-year term.

Stanford was also president of the Central Pacific Railroad and president of the Southern Pacific Company. He ran ranches and a vineyard in northern California. Eventually, he became a U.S. Senator, too. Stanford founded Leland Stanford Junior University in memory of his son, who died at age 15. He built the university on his favorite ranch at Palo Alto. He also picked the school's staff and helped develop its lesson plans. He died at Palo Alto on June 21, 1893.

Judah spent the summer of 1860 scouting and surveying in the Sierra Mountains. He searched for a good route across the rugged **terrain**. Then he had to convince investors. In all the miles between Nebraska and California, Salt Lake City was the one large town. Who would lend money to build a railroad through these mountains that few people had ever seen? In 1861, Theodore Judah found four wealthy businessmen who believed in the plan. They came to be known as the Big Four. Each man invested $15,000 in the new Central Pacific Railroad.

These railroad **tycoons** had skill in business and engineering. They also had courage, fantastic plans, and teamwork. Their names were Stanford, Huntington, Hopkins,

Union Pacific and Central Pacific crews celebrate the completion of the transcontinental railroad in May 1869 at Promontory Summit, Utah.

and Crocker. The "Big Four" rose to be the most powerful men in California: Leland Stanford, president of the Central Pacific Railroad, became governor of California; he used political influence to obtain state money and land grants for his railroad. Collis Huntington traveled east to lobby and bribe the U.S. government for grants of money and free land. Mark

Hopkins served as treasurer for the vast enterprise. Charles
Crocker managed construction of the entire Central Pacific
Railroad line. He was the overseer of the dangerous tunnel-
blasting. Crocker hired thousands of Chinese workmen in
California, and he drove his work crews to work as fast as
humans could work.

Backed by the finances of these merchants, Judah returned
east to ask the United States government for support. Until
1860, businessmen had been the main railroad investors,
people who were willing to gamble on unsettled areas of the
continent. Farmers and merchants hoped they would earn
huge profits when passenger trains and freight trains rolled
through their towns. Sometimes, investments "went up in
smoke" when con men talked people into investing money for
railroads that never existed. Some honest railroad schemes
failed due only to bad planning, stock market trends, or
competition. Now, the U.S. government decided to make a
huge investment, to encourage new towns and farms to
develop on the land along the tracks.

President Lincoln was deep in the crisis of the Civil War,
but he liked the idea: a 3,000-mile-long railroad that would
cross the entire continent. In 1862, Lincoln signed the Pacific
Railroad Act. This decreed construction of railroad lines from
coast to coast. The United States government agreed to offer
millions of acres of free land to two railroad companies.
Judah's Central Pacific Railroad would start in California and

Charles Crocker (1822–1888) was in charge of construction for the Central Pacific Railroad. His job title was general superintendent of the railroad. Under his leadership, the railroad was done seven years early.

Before he worked on the Pacific railroad, Crocker had a store in Sacramento where he sold cloth, thread, and carpet. Crocker was a member of the state legislature, too, but he gave up his business and his political career to build the railroad. After the railroad was built, Crocker helped build the Southern Pacific's rail route across the Southwest. He also built dams and helped develop California's Central Valley. He died on August 14, 1888.

construct a track going east while another huge railroad company, the Union Pacific Railroad, would construct a track heading west from Nebraska. The two long tracks would join in Utah. Linking together, they would form America's first transcontinental railroad.

Lincoln would not live to see the east and west coasts linked by the railroad. He was assassinated in April 1865. The slain president's final train journey was a 1,700 mile trip from Washington, D.C., to his home in Springfield, Illinois. The train was painted black on the outside. The train traveled for 13 days, finally arriving on May 3. It was estimated that 7 million Americans stood along the tracks to bow their heads as the funeral train passed by.

As construction began on the Union Pacific and Central Pacific railroads, the Big Four engaged in plenty of "wheeling

Two Indians watch as a small camp of men survey and prepare land for the impending railroad. Many Native Americans were unhappy with the toll the railroad construction took on the land and the bison, which were essential elements of their way of life during the 19th century.

and dealing," bribery, and wild scams. The transcontinental was an enormous railroad project. It involved hiring thousands and thousands of men: an army of laborers from Ireland, Germany, China, England, Mexico, and all the states in America. Stocks and bonds and land passed from the government into the hands of the Big Four during the six years of construction. Early in the project, Theodore Judah got into an argument

Collis Huntington (1821–1900) went to California during the Gold Rush in 1849. He was not a prospector, however. He opened a hardware store in Sacramento, selling items to the miners. His partner in the store was Mark Hopkins. It was in their store that Theodore Judah first explained his plan for the railroad to Huntington, Hopkins, Leland Stanford, and Charles Crocker— the men who became known as the Big Four.

Huntington was the vice president of the Central Pacific Railroad. One of his jobs was to sell bonds in New York, Washington, and other cities to help pay for the railroad. After the transcontinental railroad was built, he went on to buy other railroads, and he founded the town of Newport News, Virginia, as a port to which one of his railroads could send goods. Huntington died on August 13, 1900.

with his partners. The Big Four then forced Judah to sell out his stock in the **enterprise**. Traveling back east, he became sick with yellow fever. He never lived to see the completion of the vast cross-country railroad he had helped to inspire.

The Big Four acquired nine million acres of land and received millions of dollars in government contracts. In return, these four businessmen gave Americans a route across the United States. On May 10, 1869, the tracks of the Union Pacific and Central Pacific railroads were joined together at Promontory Summit, Utah. Soon, people would be able to travel across the vast country on the transcontinental railroad.

A surveyor from Scotland was another one of the brilliant railroad engineers in California. James Keddie arrived from

Mark Hopkins (1813–1878) was the Central Pacific Railroad's treasurer. Before he became Collis Huntington's partner, Hopkins owned a store in Placerville during the Gold Rush. Hopkins was a lawyer, also, and the other members of the Big Four trusted his judgment. They had him look over all their projects, and if he liked a project, the group went ahead with it. If he didn't, they backed out.

After the transcontinental railroad was done, Hopkins stayed in the railroad business. He worked for the Southern Pacific Railroad, and he died in Yuma, Arizona, on March 29, 1878, while inspecting the Sunset Route for that line.

Scotland in the 1860s. A wagon road company had hired him to explore and look for new routes for covered wagons. Keddie discovered an Indian trail that had easy grades (no steep inclines). He felt it would be perfect for rail access. In 1867, Keddie found several partners. Civil War General William Rosecrans, Creed Hammond, and Asbury Harpending joined Keddie to form the Oroville & Virginia City Railroad Company. Keddie soon learned that enthusiasm would not be enough, however, as the Central Pacific fought to compete with him. Collis Huntington was one of his competitors in Washington. Tricks and bribery were common; some railroad tycoons stopped at nothing. When the Southern Pacific was building railroads, workmen sometimes reached a town that refused to grant space to the railroad. The SPRR simply used government connections to establish a new town.

The largest railroad companies schemed to establish monopolies. They wanted to eliminate any competition, and then be free to raise rates. Favorite customers got special lower rates, while others were forced to pay more. When stagecoaches no longer drove old routes, the railroads did develop a monopoly. They offered the only rapid land transportation. Farmers were outraged to find themselves trapped into paying high prices when they needed to transport goods. Shippers and merchants then joined together to build new rail lines. In Washington, D.C., developers scrambled to win government grants.

👆 A steam engine rolls into the station, catching everyone's attention, in this advertising poster created by a midwestern railroad company. Railroad travel revolutionized the United States by making distant goods and services more readily available and providing easier access to faraway places.

IRON ROADS IN THE WEST

BY 1880, THE UNITED STATES HAD 93,000 MILES OF RAILROAD TRACK. ONLY 10 YEARS LATER, IN 1890, there were already 164,000 miles of track. Many of the lines followed the routes of the pioneers who had come earlier on foot and on horseback. The "Katy" line followed western cattle trails through Missouri, Kansas, and Texas.

North Platte, Nebraska, was a natural site where wagon trains had stopped while traveling along the Oregon Trail, the Mormon Trail, the Pony Express, or the Overland Trail. The town was founded in 1873 along Nebraska's rivers. North Platte became a stop for the Union Pacific Railroad. Today, it is still the site of the largest railroad yard in the world.

By 1881, America had a second transcontinental railroad on the ground. The Southern Pacific Railroad connected in New Mexico with the Santa Fe Railroad (known as the Atchison, Topeka, & Santa Fe Railroad). In the 1890s, the Santa Fe Railroad had 9,000 miles of track and lines that connected to Los Angeles and Chicago. The Sante Fe became one of the longest railroads in the world.

Railroad men used wild advertising tricks to lure immigrants to new towns along the railroads. In 1884, the Northern Pacific Railroad advertised overseas. It described a 1200-acre "banana belt" farm in the Dakotas! Whole communities moved from Scandinavia to America, expecting to find a tropical climate. In 1873, a railroad town on the Missouri River changed its name to Bismarck, to attract German immigrants who felt loyal to Prince Bismarck of the German Empire. American railroad advertisements captured the imagination of people around the world. By 1889, the territories of Montana, Washington, North Dakota, and South Dakota all became states due to railroad ads that brought settlers and their families.

Often, two different railroad companies would compete for the right to lay tracks over the same route. In the 1870s, who would build a line going from Colorado south to Mexico's silver mines? The Big Four wanted this route, but owners of the Atchison, Topeka, & Santa Fe Railroad claimed they had the right of way. A former Civil War general was in charge; he led the AT&SF Railroad in a bold approach. He hired "big guns" to protect the AT&SF train stations. Professional gunfighter Bat Masterson handled this job: gun battles, kidnappings, and a courtroom battle occurred before the rail companies finally settled the dispute.

By 1883, another transcontinental line led from California to New Orleans. Engineers were using brilliant, sophisticated

☞ As a boy, Andrew Carnegie moved with his family from Scotland to the United States, settling near Pittsburgh, Pennsylvania. From humble beginnings as a poor immigrant, Carnegie rose to control a steelmaking empire valued at half a billion dollars by 1899. Carnegie's steel mills turned out millions of tons of rails, wheels, bridge girders, and other items necessary for the expansion of the railroads during the second half of the 19th century.

designs to lay these tracks. The tracks crossed through rocks, sand, and forests. William Hood, Assistant Chief Engineer of the Southern Pacific Railroad, was an example of genius; he needed to plan a track for a train climbing down California's Tehachapi Mountains into the San Joaquin Valley. Skillfully, Hood designed 18 tunnels through 20 miles of steep mountain terrain.

Andrew Carnegie produced steel for the railroads using a method called the **Bessemer process**. This method had been invented in the 1850s by an Englishman named Henry Bessemer. While trying to create stronger iron, Bessemer found that by blowing oxygen through the hot "pig iron" purified the iron and helped increase its temperature, so it could be easily poured. The material that resulted—steel—was stronger, less brittle, and easier to work than iron.

In the years after the Civil War ended in 1865, there was a great demand for steel products. Steel was needed not only for railroad rails, but also for wheels, couplings, and frames for the rail cars, and for bridges to cross the rivers and chasms of the West. Carnegie started a steel company in order to help meet this demand. By 1899, the Carnegie Steel Company controlled most of the steel mills around Pittsburgh, and his mills alone were producing more steel than all the mills in Great Britain. While Andrew Carnegie did not invent the Bessemer process, he and his employees did improve furnaces for heating iron, methods for manufacturing and transporting steel equipment, and other aspects of the steel industry.

Construction continued, spreading like a web. In 1859, an American named Cyrus K. Holliday had said that steel rails could replace the wagon route known as the **Santa Fe Trail**. Construction crews began work there in 1868, tearing up the Rocky Mountains by the root. Holliday was an individual with a powerful imagination; rails now lay across old wagon trails in every direction. The Southern Pacific merged with the Central

Pacific, and competed madly with other lines. During a price war in 1887, railroad tycoons adjusted freight fares from the Midwest to southern California: from $125 down to $1. The railroad would do anything to capture more interest, more customers, more business. Wild land speculation also encouraged interest in the railroads. Who knew how much America would grow, and how many people could find their fortunes in the new railroads?

Other railroad lines were developing in the West. In 1864, the U.S. government gave the Northern Pacific Railroad a land grant of 39 million acres, the largest ever given to a railroad. The line was chartered to run from Duluth, Minnesota, to Seattle, Washington. The Northern Pacific broke a treaty with the Sioux tribe, and this led to trouble and violence. General Custer and his Seventh Cavalry tried to guard the supply wagons and **surveyors** of the Northern Pacific in the Yellowstone River Valley.

Several years later, the head of the Northern Pacific gave money to create Yellowstone National Park in Wyoming. He planned to advertise so tourists would travel by railroad to see Yellowstone Canyon in the park. The Northern Pacific Company went bankrupt in 1873, but railroad lines continued to spread across Wyoming and the West.

By the 1900s, trains could take passengers to Yellowstone, the Grand Canyon, Yosemite, and Glacier National Park.

The Sierra Nevada Mountains created a daunting obstacle for railroad engineers to overcome. Only by a dangerous system of blasting out chunks of the rock could the mountains be tamed and rails placed.

5
MORE RAILS IN CALIFORNIA

THE BIG FOUR SAW THE POTENTIAL FOR STEEL ROADS TO SPREAD THROUGHOUT CALIFORNIA. They built a Southern Pacific Railroad line from San Francisco down to San Diego. They added the Yuba Railroad line from Sacramento up to Northern California, with a **spur** traveling from Sacramento into the San Joaquin Valley. Connecting short rail lines to their longer lines, they helped develop trade lines while also enriching themselves. By 1884, the Southern Pacific Railroad owned all standard tracks in the entire state of California.

The Southern Pacific competed with the Western Pacific for every mile of the track. Their tricks included setting up fake mining companies to stake out claims along the route. The Southern Pacific and Western Pacific companies accused each other of stealing good workmen. Track workers often grumbled because wages were low. The companies sometimes hired detectives to work among the crew and investigate suspicions that a competitor might be urging workmen to change employers.

San Francisco Bay was the scene of a battle between armed railroad workers with guns. The Southern Pacific controlled the waterfront through illegal bribes to Oakland's city government. Would only one railroad have rights to enter the port? Western Pacific workmen finally muscled their way in to lay track at a terminal on the Bay. Rail work continued from San Francisco to Los Angeles and from California into Arizona, New Mexico, Texas, and Louisiana.

The workmen built the roads, but the surveyors were the trail-finders who had to discover the best paths for them to follow. Surveying was difficult work. From desert sand to mountain cliffs and canyons, there were no footpaths for safety. Surveyors had to blaze their own unmapped trails through the brush. They set up base camps and then began to clear a road for wagons to haul supplies to them. Several hundred wagons brought heavy equipment for building the railroad. In all kinds of weather, it was necessary to construct rope bridges across rivers, hack down miles of forest **timber**, drill through solid rock, and survive as campers in the wilderness.

Surveyors often traveled in secrecy. Like the gold and silver sought by miners in the west, the routes the surveyors discovered were extremely valuable. Whoever found the best route might win a government contract and the opportunity to build a lucrative new railroad line. Also, people who

👆 This photograph was taken in 1865, while President Lincoln's funeral train was on its way across the nation to his final resting place in Springfield, Illinois. Lincoln's support of the railroads facilitated their completion before his untimely death.

owned the land along the surveyed route had a chance to become wealthy, either by selling their land to the railroad or by establishing a town where the trains would stop. Someone who knew in advance the route along which a railroad company planned to build could claim the land

By the 1880s, travelers to the West could use one of 10 railroads to get where they were going. The Great Northern Route that traveled between St. Paul and Seattle was the most northern route, while the southernmost route belonged to the Southern Pacific that went between New Orleans and Los Angeles. The others were large regional lines that connected the cross-country routes.

cheaply before the company could begin working.

Because great amounts of money were at stake, the railroads were very careful to hide their activities from others. Railroad companies hired employees who were willing to work in secret for a year or more, never telling their families where they were working. Although these employees could stay in contact with families or friends, they had to send letters to the railroad company's home office. From there, the company routed the mail to the homes of the workers' families.

The planning of a railroad could continue for months—or even years—after the surveyors initially hiked through an area and mapped a route. Once the planning stages were complete, the railroaders would set to work grading the route and setting down the steel rails.

As new railroad lines were built, there was often great excitement when the first passenger train arrived in towns along the line. The entire population of the town would turn out at the station. People stood on rooftops to get a good view; they would call down to those on the ground and let them know that the train was coming into sight. Brass bands and parades greeted the train; parents and children offered watermelons and grapes to the passengers.

In 1919, when passenger service first came to Oakland, California, a four-mile-long parade welcomed the train and led the passengers to a banquet. In those years before the age of radio and television, trains provided the first high-speed social connection between people. In addition to necessary supplies, railroads transported news, fashion, and culture. The network of railroads was helping California become one of the wealthiest states in America.

👆 Although train passengers were safer from Indian attacks, they still had to contend with the danger of occasional robbers aboard the train cars. This daredevil bandit is going through every passenger on the train, making each walk ahead once they have been robbed.

LIFE ALONG THE WESTERN RAILROADS

RAILROAD COMPANIES PAID ENTIRE ARMIES OF WORKERS TO HIKE OUT INTO UNMAPPED forests, deserts and mountains. The railroads needed workers in construction crews and operating crews; crews to maintain the tracks and the bridges and the signals; managers to keep records; agents to sell tickets; skilled workmen to repair sophisticated equipment. Families sent their sons and husbands to the railroads to work at all these jobs. During the good years, these men found steady employment. They led rough lives, however. Drinking and gambling were common; often, workmen lost all their earnings in card games and fights.

Together, the workmen and the tracks sprawled westward. A culture of work seemed to follow the trains; railroads attracted people with high energy and ambition. On the Atchison, Topeka, and Santa Fe Railway in 1874, 90,000 more passengers traveled out west than returned east. Trains traveling westward also carried shipments of manufactured

This political cartoon illustrates the public's view of "robber barons" such as Edward H. Harriman. The caricature shows all of America's railroads heading into his mouth; the caption reads, "Design for a Union Station."

goods. Frequently, new tracks created new settlements, rather than merely leading to already-established settlements.

Trains traveling eastward brought shipments of America's

natural resources: coal, cattle, sheep, ore, grain, buffalo bones, and buffalo hides. Small businesses as well as large organizations saw train locomotives as a symbol of progress. From distant areas of the Southwest, farmers in the Rio Grande Valley could send their produce to eastern markets.

From remote woods in the Northwest, loggers welcomed the steam engines that transformed logging. American woodsmen led a hard and dangerous life; in the 1870s, they were still using log-strewn roadways to slide fresh logs out of the woods and into the rivers. These roadways were made of greased logs that allowed new logs to slide easily over the slippery surface. Teams of oxen dragged 80-foot logs across the roadway to the river edge. Then the huge logs floated downstream to market. By the 1880s, the logging railroads arrived in the Northwest. Steam locomotives pulled flatcars along steel rail tracks. Now, logs traveled across country by rail rather than by river.

From coast to coast, hardware stores sprang up all along the train routes. Railroad business was good for blacksmith shops, cloth shops, groceries, lumber mills, grain elevators, and more.

The railroad towns were usually far apart, however. The western railroads ran through isolated areas during the days of the Wild West. Gangs of train robbers knew that trains carried enormous sums of money to pay railroad crewmen. These gangs attacked the moving trains by unhitching the railcars from the engine, then blowing open the safes with sticks of

Butch Cassidy and his Wild Bunch were some of the most famous train robbers. The Wild Bunch robbed banks, stole cattle, and attacked trains. In 1899, they flagged down a Union Pacific train, used dynamite to blow open the safe, and escaped with $30,000.

After suffering many such train robberies, the Union Pacific finally hired professional gunmen to ride on a train. The railroad supplied these "hired guns" with rifles and horses waiting in the stock car. A detective named Charles Siringo chased the Wild Bunch for four years, from Wyoming to the state of Arkansas.

The Wild Bunch eluded the law until they posed for this photograph. Afterward, detectives made copies and circulated them to towns throughout the West. This led to the capture of several members of the gang. However, Butch Cassidy (seated at the right) and his partner Harry "The Sundance Kid" Longabaugh (seated at left) escaped to South America. They are believed to have been killed in a shootout with police in Bolivia in 1909, although some reports claim that Butch Cassidy got away, returned to the United States, and lived quietly until his death in 1937.

dynamite. Butch Cassidy, Jesse James, and the James Gang were robbers who spread fear among western travelers. Sometimes a gangster dressed as a passenger rode the train. He would take control and stop the train in a deserted spot. The waiting gang would rob every passenger before galloping away with the payroll. Texas Rangers, Pinkerton Guards, and U.S. Marshals worked to capture and arrest train robbers.

America felt both respect and envy for the wealthy men who ran the railroads. Men such as Jay Gould, James Hill, and Edward Harriman were able to **consolidate** several of the western rail lines into railroad empires. They came to be known as "railway barons." Many American farmers viewed the successful barons as "railroad pirates" who charged high prices. The Granger Movement formed to oppose high train fares for farmers' shipments of corn. The government tried to show that it did not want to favor the wealthy railroad barons; it created an Interstate Commerce Commission in 1887 and passed the Sherman Anti-Trust Act in 1890. These did not reduce the fortunes of the barons, but in the 1900s, the large railroad companies lost their power over the nation's commerce.

A Maglev train is tested at a research center in Japan. While most of the trains in the world still run on the ground, the new technology of magnetic levitation would allow the train to float above the tracks, allowing for less friction and a more efficient ride.

WESTERN RAILROADS INTO THE 20TH AND 21ST CENTURIES

BY 1916, STEAM LOCOMOTIVES WERE ROLLING ALONG MORE THAN 254,000 MILES OF AMERICAN track. Americans were used to the sight of smoke pouring from the tops of trains. In the 1920s and 1930s, however, clean electricity and clean diesel fuel began to replace coal and steam. New locomotives were quieter and did not exhale dark clouds of smoke.

The 20th century was an era of invention. Steel boxcars replaced wooden rail cars; railroad **dispatchers** could communicate on new two-way radios; passenger cars offered reclining seats and other comforts. New designs and materials were modernizing the railroad business. At the same time, however, the nation began to construct a new kind of road: the highway.

In the 1800s, railroads had not faced much competition

Early locomotives burned wood or coal to create steam energy, and trainmen had to be on board to keep fueling the engine. Rudolph Diesel, a German engineer, invented a new locomotive engine in 1892. His Diesel engines used oil for fuel, and they did not need as much supervision as coal-burning engines. By 1925, a diesel engine ran on an American track in New Jersey.

from other land transportation. In the 1900s, however, railroads suddenly had to compete with automobiles and also with airplanes. These new inventions offered privacy, independence, and speed. Like the canal operators and stagecoach operators who came before them, railroad operators wished that they could halt progress. Everyone in America seemed to want a car; how could railroads survive?

Many railroads joined together or bought up other lines. Some lines, like the Milwaukee line, went out of business. The Milwaukee Road had been completed in 1909. Sixty thousand people traveled on this line in the following years, to settle farmland and ranchland in Montana. But by 1924, after several years of drought, the Milwaukee line owed $444 million in debts. It declared bankruptcy.

Each railroad closing meant that many employees lost their jobs. Railroad closings often caused town closings, as well; after all, if trains stopped arriving, people moved away. Lively railroad communities became ghost towns.

Many of the railways built in the last century are still useful in modern times. This long Burlington Northern-Santa Fe train transports goods from New Mexico to California using a road originally built by the Atchiston, Topeka & Santa Fe Railroad in the 1880s.

American trains now use a technique called "piggybacking" to make it easier to load and unload freight shipments from a train onto a truck or another type of shipper.

During World War I, the U.S. government seized control of the railroads. During World War II, the government relied on the railroads again; soldiers and military equipment traveled on the tracks during the 1940s. One generation later, in the 1970s, the U.S. government formed Amtrak and Conrail. Today these railroad corporations operate passenger and freight trains. The nation's rail systems are still struggling to succeed.

There are some hopes, however. In April 2001, Amtrak started a high-speed rail line between Boston and Washington, D.C. The line, which made stops at New York, Philadelphia, Baltimore, and other important cities along the way, was immediately popular. After the terrorist attack on the World Trade Center in September 2001, many people started talking about expanding rail service as a way to ease the overcrowding of airline flights.

Another possibility for the future are magnetically levitated trains, called **Maglev** trains. These trains do not rest on iron rails with steel wheels, as current trains do. Instead, two powerful magnetic fields, one created by the train and another by the guideway, repel each other, enabling the train to float over the guidelines. Because the trains do not have wheels that run along the tracks, there is no friction. This allows Maglev trains to reach very high speeds—as much as 300 miles per hour.

Maglev trains have been running in Japan since the 1970s, and a Japanese train set a speed record of 344 miles per hour in 1998. In Germany, a Maglev train line is being built between Hamburg and Berlin; it is expected to be completed in 2005. A downside to Maglev trains is the great cost of constructing the guideways; in the United States, it may cost between $10 and $12 million per mile to build a Maglev route.

Although it may be many years before the first Maglev train route is built in the United States, some day in the near future the railroad era in the West may begin again as high-speed trains race across the country where iron rails stretched more than a century ago.

GLOSSARY

Artery

A blood vessel that is part of the system carrying blood under pressure from the heart to the rest of the body; a main route in a road or rail system.

Avalanche

A large mass of snow or rock falling down a mountainside.

Bessemer Process

A process of making steel out of pig iron.

Boom

Widespread expansion in sales and economic activity.

Charter

A grant of rights from the government.

Commerce

Business; buying and selling of goods.

Conduit

A channel through which things move along.

Consolidate

To join together into one whole.

Dispatchers

Railroad officials who schedule departures.

Enterprise

A business organization or project.

Gold Rush

Time of feverish search for gold in California, beginning in 1848.

Locomotive

A self-propelled vehicle that runs on rails and is used to move railroad cars.

Maglev

High-speed train that travels on magnetic cushions (magnetic levitation).

Persevere

To keep doing something or working at something, in spite of difficulties.

Santa Fe Trail

Important wagon train route from Missouri to Santa Fe, New Mexico.

Spur

A side branch of a railroad line.

Surveyors

People who precisely measure an area of land.

Tedious

Tiresome, boring.

Terrain

The physical features of an area of land.

Timber

The wood of a tree.

Toiled

Worked terribly hard on a difficult job.

Trestles

Frameworks of timbers or steel for carrying a railroad over any size ditch.

Turnpike

A toll road.

Tycoons

Businessmen of great wealth and power.

Utility

Usefulness of something.

1781

George Stephenson invents a steam-powered traveling machine.

1823

Stephenson invents an iron track for his steam-powered car.

1827

The Baltimore and Ohio railroad, the first major rail line in the United States, is established.

1830

Peter Cooper's Tom Thumb becomes the first American-built steam locomotive.

1844

Samuel B. Morse sends the world's first telegram over a telegraph line along the B&O Railroad right-of-way.

1852

The first railroad line west of the Mississippi, the Pacific Railroad of Missouri, is opened.

1853

A New York to Chicago railroad line is established.

1859

The first Pullman sleeping car travels overnight between cities in Illinois.

1858

A Philadelphia to Chicago railroad line is opened.

1861

The Civil War begins, slowing railroad construction in the United States.

1867

The first mail car is used on the Chicago & Northwestern Line.

1869

In May the transcontinental railroad is completed when four ceremonial spikes—two gold, one silver, and one made of silver, gold, and iron—are hammered into the track at Promontory Summit, Utah.

1877

The first major railroad strike occurs.

1892

The diesel engine is invented.

FURTHER READING

Ambrose, Stephen. *Nothing Like It In the World: The Men Who Built the Transcontinental Railroad 1863–1869*. New York: Simon and Schuster, 2000.

Bain, David. *Empire Express: Building the First Transcontinental Railroad*. New York: Viking, 1999.

Durbin, William. *The Journal of Sean Sullivan: A Transcontinental Railroad Worker*. New York: Scholastic, 1999.

Fraser, Mary Ann. *Ten Mile Day and the Building of the Transcontinental Railroad*. New York: Henry Holt Publishers, 1996.

Gregory, Kristiana. *The Great Railroad Race: The Diary of Libby West*. New York: Scholastic, 1999.

Kalman, Bobbie. *The Railroad*. New York: Crabtree Publishing, 1999.

Krensky, Stephen. *The Iron Dragon Never Sleeps*. New York: Bantam Dell Doubleday Books for Young Readers, 1994.

McCarter, Steve. *Guide to the Milwaukee Road in Montana*. Helena: Montana Historical Society, 1992.

Spangenburg, Ray, and Diane Moser. *The Story of America's Railroads*. New York: Facts on File, 1991.

Ward, Geoffrey. *The West: An Illustrated History*. Boston: Little, Brown and Company, 1996.

Yep, Laurence. *Dragon's Gate*. New York: Harpercollins Juvenile Books, 1993.

INTERNET RESOURCES

Information about railroads of the West

http://www.over-land.com/rrwest.html

http://cprr.org/faster.html

http://xroads.virginia.edu/~MA96/RAILROAD/intro.html

http://www.over-land.com/rrgauge.html

http://history.cc.ukans.edu/heritage/research/rr/railroads.html

http://www.thehistorynet.com/WildWest/articles/2000/08002_2text.htm

http://www.frontiertrails.com/oldwest/railroads.html

http://homepage.interaccess.com/~dreyfus/history.html

http://www.americanwest.com/

http://web.uccs.edu/~history/index/west.html

Information about the Transcontinental Railroad

http://www.nps.gov/gosp

http://www.cprr.com/faster.html

http://www.uprr.com/uprr/ffh/history

http://www.csrmf.org/transbuild.html

INDEX

PHOTO CREDITS

ABOUT THE AUTHOR

Hannah Strauss Magram is a graduate of Barnard College. Her work appears in numerous publications including *The Baltimore Sun*, *First Things Journal of Religion & Public Life*, and *Response Contemporary Review*. She and her husband live in Maryland with their three children.

◆ON THE◆ HORIZON

Grateful acknowledgment is made to the following publishers, authors, and agents for their permission to reprint copyrighted material. Any adaptations are noted in the individual acknowledgments and are made with the full knowledge and approval of the authors or their representatives. Every effort has been made to locate all copyright proprietors; any errors or omissions in copyright notice are inadvertent and will be corrected in future printings as they are discovered.

"Ali Baba Bernstein" excerpt adapted from *The Adventures of Ali Baba Bernstein* by Johanna Hurwitz. Text copyright © 1985 by Johanna Hurwitz. By permission of William Morrow & Co.

Amy's Goose by Efner Tudor Holmes, illustrated by Tasha Tudor. (Thomas Y. Crowell) Copyright © 1977 by Efner Tudor Holmes. Illustrations copyright © 1977 by Tasha Tudor. Adapted and reprinted by permission of Harper & Row, Publishers, Inc.

"April Rain Song" from *The Dream Keeper and Other Poems* by Langston Hughes. Copyright 1932 by Alfred A. Knopf, Inc. and renewed 1960 by Langston Hughes. Reprinted by permission of Alfred A. Knopf, Inc., and of the author's agents, Harold Ober Associates Incorporated.

"Beethoven's Biggest Fan" from "Peanuts" by Charles Schulz. Reprinted by permission of United Feature Syndicate, Inc.

The Big Orange Splot written and illustrated by Daniel Manus Pinkwater. Copyright © 1977 by Daniel Manus Pinkwater. Reprinted by permission of Scholastic Inc.

Acknowledgments continue on pages 382–383, which constitute an extension of this copyright page.

WORLD
OF
READING

◆ ON THE ◆
HORIZON

P. DAVID PEARSON   DALE D. JOHNSON

THEODORE CLYMER   ROSELMINA INDRISANO   RICHARD L. VENEZKY

JAMES F. BAUMANN   ELFRIEDA HIEBERT   MARIAN TOTH

Consulting Authors

CARL GRANT   JEANNE PARATORE

SILVER BURDETT & GINN

NEEDHAM, MA • MORRISTOWN, NJ
ATLANTA, GA • CINCINNATI, OH • DALLAS, TX
MENLO PARK, CA • NORTHFIELD, IL

ONE OF A KIND

GATHER 'ROUND _____ 100

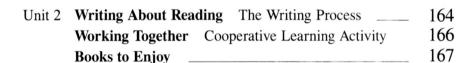

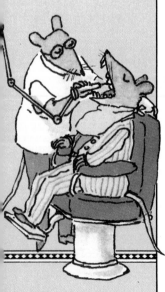

WORKING IT OUT

168

Weather or Not

ONE
OF A
KIND

Everyone is special in some way.

What makes some people special to read about?

COCHITI STORYTELLERS,
Pueblo pottery by Rita Lewis, Helen Cordero, Ada Suina, American, 1964

Mr. Plumbean just wants to be himself.
For some reason, this upsets the neighbors.

The Big Orange

written and illustrated by
Daniel Manus Pinkwater

Mr. Plumbean lived on a street where all the houses were the same.

He liked it that way. So did everybody else on Mr. Plumbean's street. "This is a neat street," they would say. Then one day . . .

A sea gull flew over Mr. Plumbean's house. He was carrying a can of bright orange paint. (No one knows why.) And he dropped the can (no one knows why) right over Mr. Plumbean's house.

It made a big orange splot on Mr. Plumbean's house.

"Ooooh! Too bad!" everybody said. "Mr. Plumbean will have to paint his house again."

14

"I suppose I will," said Mr. Plumbean. But he didn't paint his house right away. He looked at the big orange splot for a long time; then he went about his business.

The neighbors got tired of seeing that big orange splot. Someone said, "Mr. Plumbean, we wish you'd get around to painting your house."

"OK," said Mr. Plumbean.

He got some blue paint and some white paint, and that night he got busy. He painted at night because it was cooler.

When the paint was gone, the roof was blue. The walls were white. And the big orange splot was still there.

Then he got some more paint. He got red paint, yellow paint, green paint, and purple paint.

In the morning the other people on the street came out of their houses. Their houses were all the same. But Mr. Plumbean's house was like a rainbow. It was like a jungle. It was like an explosion.

15

There was the big orange splot. And there were little orange splots. There were stripes. There were pictures of elephants and lions and steam shovels.

The people said, "Plumbean has popped his cork, flipped his wig, blown his stack, and dropped his stopper." They went away muttering.

That day Mr. Plumbean bought carpenter's tools. That night he built a tower on top of his roof, and he painted a clock on the tower.

The next day the people said, "Plumbean has gushed his mush and lost his marbles." They decided they would pretend not to notice.

That very night Mr. Plumbean got a truck full of green things. He planted palm trees, baobabs, thorn bushes, onions, and frangipani. In the morning he bought a hammock and an alligator.

When the other people came out of their houses, they saw Mr. Plumbean swinging in a hammock between two palm trees. They saw an alligator lying in the grass. Mr. Plumbean was drinking lemonade.

"Plumbean has gone too far!"

"This used to be a neat street!"

"Plumbean, what have you done to your house?" the people shouted.

"My house is me and I am it. My house is where I like to be and it looks like all my dreams," Mr. Plumbean said.

The people went away. They asked the man who lived next door to Mr. Plumbean to go and have a talk with him. "Tell him that we all liked it here before he changed his house. Tell him that his house has to be the same as ours so we can have a neat street."

The man went to see Mr. Plumbean that evening. They sat under the palm trees drinking lemonade and talking all night long.

Early the next morning the man went out to get lumber and rope and nails and paint. When the people came out of their houses they saw a red and yellow ship next door to the house of Mr. Plumbean.

"What have you done to your house?" they shouted at the man.

"My house is me and I am it. My house is where I like to be and it looks like all my dreams," said the man, who had always loved ships.

"He's just like Plumbean!" the people said. "He's got bees in his bonnet, bats in his belfry, and knots in his noodle!"

Then, one by one, they went to see Mr. Plumbean, late at night. They would sit under the palm trees and drink lemonade and talk about their dreams—and whenever anybody visited Mr. Plumbean's house, the very next day that person would set about changing his own house to fit his dreams.

Whenever a stranger came to the street of Mr. Plumbean and his neighbors, the stranger would say, "This is not a neat street."

Then all the people would answer, "Our street is us and we are it. Our street is where we like to be, and it looks like all our dreams."

◆ LIBRARY LINK ◆

If you would like to read more books by Daniel Manus Pinkwater, look in the library for Blue Moose, Fat Men from Space, *or* Roger's Umbrella.

Reader's Response

Which would you like better—the neat street or the new street? Tell why.

The Big Orange SPLOT

 ## Questions

1. Why didn't Mr. Plumbean paint his house right away?
2. Tell what Mr. Plumbean did to improve his dream house.
3. How did the people on the street feel about Mr. Plumbean at first? What clues told you this?
4. What do you think Mr. Plumbean and his neighbor talked about all night long?
5. How do you think the people on the street behaved after all the houses were painted?

 ## Writing to Learn

THINK AND IMAGINE   Mr. Plumbean's house looks like all his dreams. Draw a picture of a house that looks as if it were made for you. Label the parts of your house.

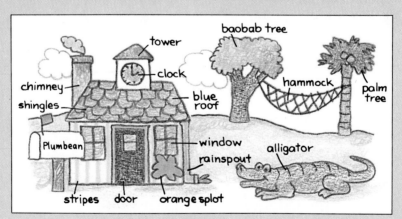

WRITE   Pretend you are living in your imaginary house on Mr. Plumbean's street. Write to describe what you might see as you approach your new home.

A Strategy for Thinking:

Making an Alike-and-Different Chart

How can you have a better understanding of the stories that you read? One good way is to make a chart that shows the likenesses and differences of the characters you read about.

Learning the Strategy

Sometimes in a story you meet a character who reminds you of someone in another story. Maybe they both have red hair, or are good at sports, or get into trouble all the time.

It is also possible that the character will remind you of a real-life person. You can compare the ways in which a real-life person and a story character are alike and different. These kinds of comparisons will give you a better understanding of stories that you read.

Using the Strategy

Read the paragraphs on the next page about Ray and Alex. Then complete the chart. Some of their likenesses and differences are already recorded.

Alex is big for his age. And that's helpful because he likes to play football. Alex does yard work every Saturday. Alex has a dog, two sisters, and thirty-nine baseball cards.

Ray's mother always wants him to eat a big breakfast. She tells him, "Your little brother is going to be bigger than you are." Ray isn't too worried. His favorite sport is bike riding—you don't have to be big to be good at that. On Saturday Ray helps at his father's fast-food shop. His favorite job is taking the orders from the customers. Ray has a cat, two sisters, a brother, and a rock collection.

Alike-and-Different Chart	
How are Alex and Ray alike?	**How are Alex and Ray different?**
1. Both have sisters. 2. Both have pets. 3. 4.	1. Ray has a brother. 2. Ray has a cat; Alex has a dog. 3. 4.

Complete the chart on your own paper. What have you learned about Alex and Ray? How did the chart help you?

Applying the Strategy to the Next Story

In the next story you will meet Miss Rumphius. As you read you will be asked to make an alike-and-different chart.

The writing connection can be found on page 39.

For many years, Miss Rumphius wondered what she could do to make the world more beautiful.

Miss Rumphius

written and illustrated
by Barbara Cooney

The Lupine (Flower) Lady lives in a small house overlooking the sea. In between the rocks around her house grow blue and purple and rose-colored flowers. The Lupine Lady is little and old. But she has not always been that way. I know. She is my great-aunt, and she told me so.

Once upon a time she was a little girl named Alice, who lived in a city by the sea. From the front steps she could see the wharves and the masts of tall ships. Many years ago her grandfather had come to America on a large sailing ship.

   In America, he worked in the shop at the bottom
of his house. He made figureheads for the prows of
ships, and carved Indians out of wood. For Alice's
grandfather was an artist. He painted pictures, too, of
sailing ships and places across the sea. When he was
very busy, Alice helped him by painting the skies in
the pictures.

23

In the evening, Alice sat on her grandfather's knee and listened to his stories of faraway places. When he had finished, Alice would say, "When I grow up, I too will go to faraway places, and when I grow old, I too will live beside the sea."

"That is all very well, little Alice," said her grandfather, "but there is a third thing you must do."

"What is that?" asked Alice.

"You must do something to make the world more beautiful," said her grandfather.

"All right," said Alice. But she did not know what that could be.

In the meantime, Alice got up and washed her face and ate porridge for breakfast. She went to school and came home and did her homework. <<◆>>

And pretty soon she was grown up.

<<◆>>

Do you know anybody like Alice? How are Alice and the person alike? How are they different?

Then my Great-aunt Alice set out to do the three things she had told her grandfather she was going to do. She left home and went to live in another city far from the sea and the salt air. There she worked in a library, dusting books and keeping them from getting mixed up, and helping people find the ones they wanted. Some of the books told her about faraway places.

People called her Miss Rumphius now.

Sometimes she went to the conservatory in the middle of the park. When she stepped inside on a wintry day, the warm moist air wrapped itself around her, and the sweet smell of jasmine flowers filled her nose.

"This is almost like a tropical island," said Miss Rumphius. "But not quite."

So Miss Rumphius went to a real tropical island, where people kept cockatoos and monkeys as pets. She walked on long beaches, picking up beautiful shells. One day she met the Bapa Raja (bä′pu rä′ju), king of a fishing village. ◄◆►

◄◆►
Do you know anybody who has gone on adventures like Miss Rumphius? How are Miss Rumphius and the person alike?

25

"You must be tired," he said. "Come into my house and rest."

So Miss Rumphius went in and met the Bapa Raja's wife. The Bapa Raja himself fetched a green coconut and cut a slice off the top so that Miss Rumphius could drink the coconut water inside. Before she left, the Bapa Raja gave her a beautiful mother-of-pearl shell on which he had painted a bird of paradise and the words, "You will always remain in my heart."

"You will always remain in mine too," said Miss Rumphius.

My great-aunt Miss Alice Rumphius climbed tall mountains where the snow never melted. She went through jungles and across deserts. She saw lions playing and kangaroos jumping. And everywhere she made friends she would never forget. Finally she came to the land of the Lotus-Eaters, and there, getting off a camel, she hurt her back.

"What a foolish thing to do," said Miss Rumphius. "Well, I have certainly seen faraway places. Maybe it is time to find my place by the sea."

And it was, and she did.

From the porch of her new house, Miss Rumphius watched the sun come up; she watched it cross the heavens and sparkle on the water; and she saw it set in glory in the evening. She started a little garden among the rocks that surrounded her house, and she planted a few flower seeds in the stony ground. Miss Rumphius was *almost* perfectly happy.

"But there is still one more thing I have to do," she said. "I have to do something to make the world more beautiful."

But what? "The world already is pretty nice," she thought, looking out over the ocean.

The next spring Miss Rumphius was not very well. Her back was bothering her again, and she had to stay in bed most of the time.

Do you know anybody who lives by the sea?
How is that person like Miss Rumphius?

The flowers she had planted the summer before had come up and bloomed in spite of the stony ground. She could see them from her bedroom window, blue and purple and rose-colored.

"Lupines," said Miss Rumphius with satisfaction. "I have always loved lupines the best. I wish I could plant more seeds this summer so that I could have still more flowers next year."

But she was not able to.

After a hard winter spring came. Miss Rumphius was feeling much better. Now she could take walks again. One afternoon she started to go up and over the hill, where she had not been in a long time.

"I don't believe my eyes!" she cried when she got to the top. For there on the other side of the hill was a large patch of blue and purple and rose-colored lupines!

"It was the wind," she said as she knelt in delight. "It was the wind that brought the seeds from my garden here! And the birds must have helped!"

Then Miss Rumphius had a wonderful idea!

She hurried home and got out her seed catalogues. She sent off to the very best seed house for five bushels of lupine seed.

All that summer Miss Rumphius, her pockets full of seeds, wandered over fields and headlands, sowing lupines. She scattered seeds along the highways and down the country lanes. She flung handfuls of them around the schoolhouse and back of the church. She tossed them into hollows and along stone walls.

Her back didn't hurt her any more at all.

The next spring there were lupines everywhere. Fields and hillsides were covered with blue and purple and rose-colored flowers. They bloomed along the highways and down the lanes. Bright patches lay around the schoolhouse and back of the church. Down in the hollows and along the stone walls grew the beautiful flowers.

29

Miss Rumphius had done the third, the most difficult thing of all!

My Great-aunt Alice, Miss Rumphius, is very old now. Her hair is very white. Every year there are more and more lupines. Now they call her the Lupine Lady. Sometimes my friends stand with me outside her gate, curious to see the old, old lady who planted the fields of lupines. When she invites us in, my friends come slowly.

They think she is the oldest woman in the world. Often she tells us stories of faraway places.

"When I grow up," I tell her, "I too will go to faraway places and come home to live by the sea."

"That is all very well, little Alice," says my aunt, "but there is a third thing you must do."

"What is that?" I ask.

"You must do something to make the world more beautiful."

"All right," I say.

But I do not know yet what that can be.

Do you know anybody who has made the world more beautiful? How is that person like Miss Rumphius? How is he or she different?

◆ LIBRARY LINK ◆

To learn more about growing flowers, read This Year's Garden *by Cynthia Rylant.*

Reader's Response

What do you think of the way Miss Rumphius lived her life? Explain your answer.

Miss Rumphius

 ## Questions

1. Who is telling the story? How do you know?
2. What were the three things that Great-aunt Alice wanted to do when she grew up?
3. Which of the three things was most difficult to do? Why?
4. How did Miss Rumphius finally solve her problem?
5. What do you think little Alice learned from Miss Rumphius?

 ## Writing to Learn

THINK AND PLAN   When Miss Rumphius was a little girl, she decided on three goals. She accomplished each of them. Read Miss Rumphius's goals below. Then plan three goals for yourself.

Miss Rumphius Made a Plan.	What Is Your Plan?
• I will go to faraway places.	• I will _____ _____.
• I will live beside the sea.	• I will _____ _____.
• I will make the world more beautiful.	• I will _____ _____.

WRITE   Choose the goal for yourself that you like best. Write about how you will reach that goal.

*Mi Dori is a talented musician. Even when things go
wrong, she makes sure that the music does not stop.*

Mi Dori

by Helen Breen

It was a hot summer night in Tanglewood,
Massachusetts. The Boston Symphony Orchestra was
getting ready to play outside on the lawn under the evening
sky. Music lovers were there to stretch out on the grass and
enjoy the music. It was so hot that July night that the
members of the orchestra had taken off their jackets and left
them behind the stage. Then they walked on stage and sat
down. The famous conductor and composer, Leonard
Bernstein, stepped in front of the orchestra. He looked at
the violin soloist for the evening, fourteen-year-old Mi Dori
Goto (mē dō′re gō′tō). Then he raised his baton and the
music began.

The orchestra was playing Serenade, a musical selection that Mr. Bernstein had written. Both Mr. Bernstein and the members of the orchestra had pages of music in front of them. Only Mi Dori played her part from memory. As Mi Dori played, the sound of beautiful music filled the night air.

Then suddenly, one of the strings on Mi Dori's violin broke. Quickly, Mi Dori turned to the violinist seated behind her. He handed her his violin. She took it and continued playing. Within a minute, another string broke. Mi Dori turned a second time to the violinist behind her. She hoped that he had put a new string on her violin, but he hadn't. All of his extra strings were offstage in his jacket pocket. Another violinist gave Mi Dori his violin. Mi Dori continued playing without making a mistake. When the music ended, the audience, Mr. Bernstein, and the members of the orchestra cheered Mi Dori.

Several thousand people had watched this young musician change violins twice in the middle of a difficult musical piece. Never once did she forget her place in the music. Everyone was amazed.

Not only had Mi Dori changed violins twice, she had played two violins she had never before touched. Those violins were much larger than her own. Because Mi Dori was so small, her violin was smaller than those played by the other musicians. The violinists in the orchestra were amazed at the way she had switched violin sizes and never hit a wrong note.

The day after the Tanglewood concert, newspapers around the United States told the story. Mi Dori's picture was on the front page of *The New York Times*. Reporters were eager to talk to her. They wanted to know how she felt when the strings on the violins broke. Was she scared? Mi Dori replied, "What could I do? My strings broke, and I didn't want to stop the music."

Mi Dori has loved music since she was a little girl. She began playing the violin when she was only four years old. Mi Dori's mother, Sietsu Goto (sāt' sōo gō' tō), was a violinist, too. She knew, even when Mi Dori was very young, that Mi Dori had a special talent. Mi Dori and her mother lived in Japan at that time. When a famous American violin teacher, Dorothy DeLay, was visiting Japan, Mrs. Goto sent her a tape of Mi Dori's violin playing.

Conductor Leonard Bernstein congratulates Mi Dori.

Ms. DeLay listened to the tape and thought that Mi Dori's playing was "extraordinary." Ms. DeLay wanted Mi Dori and her mother to come to the United States so that Mi Dori could study with her in New York. Even though it was hard to leave their home in Japan, Mi Dori and her mother decided to move to New York. Mi Dori was eleven at the time.

Mi Dori now attends the Professional Children's School in New York City. Most of her classmates there are actors and actresses. Mi Dori says that school in the United States is different from school in Japan. "I never knew any actors and actresses in Japan, and now I see lots of my friends on television."

Besides going to school, Mi Dori practices the violin four to five hours a day. She takes extra classes at Juilliard, the most famous music school in the country. She also plays the piano and the viola. Mi Dori studies the piano because it is required at Juilliard. But she plays the viola, which is like a large violin, just because she likes it.

Mi Dori enjoys many other things besides music. When she was eight, Mi Dori saw a TV show about the Inca, people of South America who lived long ago. She began to read all she could about the Inca. Mi Dori says that she might like to learn more about the Inca when she is older. She also likes to write stories and says she may become a writer. Despite her fame, Mi Dori likes to do many of the same things that you like to do. "I like to skip rope. I like to jog a little, watch television, and read." She also likes to play with her cat and listen to popular music.

Mi Dori relaxes after violin practice.

Some people would say that Mi Dori's life is anything but ordinary. At the age of eleven she was the guest soloist with the Philadelphia Orchestra. When Mi Dori came to rehearsal on the day of the concert, she looked out into the audience to make sure her teacher, Ms. DeLay, was there. Then she began to play the violin. Irvin Rosen, the leading violinist of the orchestra, described the way Mi Dori played: "If I practiced three thousand years, I couldn't play like that. None of us could." That evening, when Mi Dori finished her violin piece, the audience jumped to their feet and cheered. Four times Mi Dori left the stage, but the audience kept calling her back.

Mi Dori has been on television several times in programs about young musicians. She was also in a TV special, "Christmas at the White House," where she performed for the President. Mi Dori has traveled throughout the United States and Europe to perform with well-known orchestras. Everywhere, music reviewers praise Mi Dori's violin playing.

Mi Dori has an extraordinary talent. She plays difficult music very well. She is also a strong performer, able to go on with the show even when things go wrong. Her audiences know that they are listening to one of the best violinists of any age when Mi Dori plays. Surely, Mi Dori is one of a kind.

Reader's Response

Mi Dori has been famous since she was very young. Would you like to be famous? What would you like about it? What wouldn't you like?

Mi Dori

 ## Questions

1. What did Mi Dori do when her violin strings broke during the Tanglewood concert?
2. Why do you think the audience, the conductor, and the orchestra cheered Mi Dori?
3. What is unusual about Mi Dori's school? How did you arrive at your answer?
4. What words might describe Mi Dori and her life?
5. Which of Mi Dori's experiences do you think is the most exciting?

 ## Writing to Learn

THINK AND COMPARE   Think of someone you know who reminds you of Mi Dori. Look at the Alike-and-Different Chart below. Then copy it and complete it.

Alike-and-Different Chart
How are Mi Dori and the person alike?
1. _____
2. _____
3. _____
How are Mi Dori and the person different?
1. _____
2. _____
3. _____

WRITE   Write sentences about the person. Tell how this person is like Mi Dori and different from her.

READING
NON-FICTION

Comprehension:
Sequence

The order in which things happen is called sequence. Knowing the sequence of events helps you understand and enjoy what you are reading. In other words, a story makes more sense when you know when things happen.

Do you remember these events from the story "Mi Dori"?

Mi Dori played with the Boston Symphony Orchestra when she was fourteen.

Mi Dori began playing the violin when she was four.

When Mi Dori was eleven, she and her mother moved to New York.

Although all these statements are true, they really happened in a different order. Can you put them in the right order? What clues will help you figure out the right order?

Making a Flow Chart

One way to help you understand sequence is to draw a flow chart. If you made a flow chart for these events in Mi Dori's life, it would look like this:

Mi Dori began playing the violin when she was four.

When Mi Dori was eleven, she and her mother moved to New York.

Mi Dori played with the Boston Symphony Orchestra when she was fourteen.

Sometimes an author will use clue words such as *first, next,* and *finally* to show sequence. At other times, you have to figure out the sequence on your own. As you read, ask yourself, "What happened first? Then what happened?"

Using What You Have Learned

Make a flow chart of the events in this paragraph from "Mi Dori."

Then suddenly, one of the strings on Mi Dori's violin broke. Quickly, Mi Dori turned to the violinist seated behind her. He handed her his violin. She took it and continued playing. Within a minute, another string broke. . . . Another violinist gave Mi Dori his violin.

As You Read

As you read "Ali Baba Bernstein," think about the sequence of events and why the sequence is important.

Ali Baba Bernstein

by Johanna Hurwitz

Most of us share a name with someone else, but David Bernstein wants a name all to himself—a one-of-a-kind name.

David Bernstein was eight years, five months, and seventeen days old when he chose his new name.

There were already four Davids in David Bernstein's third-grade class. Every time his teacher, Mrs. Booxbaum, called, "David," all four boys answered. David didn't like that one bit. He wished he had an exciting name like one of the explorers he learned about in social studies—Vasco Da Gama. Once he found two unusual names on a program his parents brought home from a concert—Zubin Mehta (zōō'bin mā' tə) and Wolfgang Amadeus Mozart (vôlf'gäᴎgk ä' mä dā' ƆƆs mō'tsärt). Now those were names with pizzazz!

David Bernstein might have gone along forever being just another David if it had not been for the book report that his teacher assigned.

"I will give extra credit for fat books," Mrs. Booxbaum told the class.

She didn't realize that all of her students would try to outdo one another. That afternoon when the third grade went to the school library, everyone tried to find the fattest book.

Melanie found a book with eighty pages.

Sam found a book with ninety-seven pages.

Jeffrey found a book with one hundred nineteen pages.

David K. and David S. each took a copy of the same book. It had one hundred forty-five pages.

None of the books was long enough for David Bernstein. He found one that had two hundred fourteen pages. But he wanted a book that had more pages than the total of all the pages in all the books his classmates were reading. He wanted to be the best student in the class—even in the entire school.

That afternoon he asked his mother what the fattest book was. "I guess that would have to be the Manhattan telephone book," she said.

David Bernstein rushed to get the phone book. He lifted it up and opened to the last page. When he saw that it had over 1,578 pages, he was delighted.

He knew that no student in the history of P.S. 35 had ever read such a fat book. Just think how much extra credit he would get! David took the book and began to read name after name after name. After turning through all the A pages, he skipped to the name Bernstein. He found the listing for his father, Robert Bernstein. There were fifteen of them. Then he counted the number of David Bernsteins in the telephone book. There were seventeen. Right at that moment, David Bernstein decided two things: he would change his name and he would find another book to read.

The next day David went back to the school library. He asked the librarian to help him pick out a very fat book. "It must be very exciting, too," he told her.

"I know just the thing for you," said the librarian.

She handed David a thick book with a bright red cover. It was *The Arabian Nights*. It had only three hundred thirty-seven pages, but it looked a lot more interesting than the phone book. When he showed the book to his teacher the next day, she was very pleased.

"That is a good book," she said. "David, you have made a fine choice."

It was at that moment that David Bernstein announced his new name. He had found it in the library book.

"From now on," David said, "I want to be called Ali Baba Bernstein."

Mrs. Booxbaum was surprised. David's parents were even more surprised. "David is a beautiful name," said his mother. "It was my grandfather's name."

"You can't just go around changing your name when you feel like it," his father said. "How will I ever know who I'm talking to?"

"You'll know it's still me," Ali Baba told his parents.

Mr. and Mrs. Bernstein finally agreed, although both of them often forgot and called their son David.

So now in Mrs. Booxbaum's class, there were three Davids and one Ali Baba. Ali Baba Bernstein was very happy. He was sure that a boy with an exciting name would have truly exciting adventures.

Only time would tell.

When Ali Baba Bernstein was eight years, eleven months, and four days old, his mother asked him how he wanted to celebrate his ninth birthday. He could take his friends to the bowling alley or to a movie. Or he could have a roller-skating party. None of these choices seemed very exciting to Ali Baba. Ali Baba wanted to do something different.

"Do you remember when I counted all the David Bernsteins in the telephone book?"

Mrs. Bernstein nodded.

"I want to invite them here for my birthday," said David.

"But you don't know them," his mother said. "And they are not your age."

"I want to see what they are all like," said Ali Baba. "If I can't invite them, then I don't want to have any party at all."

47

That night Ali Baba's parents talked about the David Bernstein party. Mr. Bernstein liked his son's idea. He thought the other David Bernsteins might be curious to meet one another. So it was agreed that Ali Baba would have the party he wanted.

The very next morning, which was Saturday, Ali Baba and his father went to his father's office. Ali Baba had written an invitation to the David Bernstein party.

Dear David Bernstein:

I found your name in the Manhattan telephone book. My name is David Bernstein, too. I want to meet all the David Bernsteins in New York. I am having a party on Friday, May 12th at 7:00 P.M., and I hope you can come.

My mother is cooking supper. She is a good cook.

> Yours truly,
> David Bernstein
> (also known as Ali Baba Bernstein)

P.S. May 12th is my ninth birthday, but you don't have to bring a present. RSVP: 555–3579

Ali Baba was going to use the computer in his father's office to print the letter. It took him a long time to type his letter on the machine. His father tried to help him, but he did not type very well either. When the letter was finally completed and the print button pushed, the machine made seventeen perfect copies—one for each David Bernstein.

That evening Ali Baba addressed the seventeen envelopes so that the invitations could be mailed on Monday morning. His father supplied the stamps. By the end of the week, two David Bernsteins had already called to say that they would come.

Ali Baba and his mother chose the menu for his birthday dinner. There would be pot roast, corn (Ali Baba's favorite vegetable), rolls, applesauce, and salad.

The evening of the party finally arrived. Ali Baba had decided to wear a pair of slacks, a sport jacket, and real dress shoes. It was not at all the way he would have dressed for a bowling party.

Ali Baba was surprised when the first guest arrived in a jogging suit and running shoes.

"How do you do," he said when Ali Baba opened the door. "I'm David Bernstein."

"Of course," said the birthday boy. "Call me Ali Baba."

Soon the living room was filled with David
Bernsteins. They ranged in age from exactly nine
years and three hours old to seventy-six years old.
There was a television director, a delicatessen owner,
a mailman, an animal groomer, a dentist, a high-
school teacher, and a writer. They all lived in
Manhattan now, but they had been born in Brooklyn,
the Bronx, Michigan, Poland, Germany, and South
Africa. None of them had ever met any of the others
before.

"I have always had trouble remembering names,"
the seventy-six-year-old David Bernstein told Ali Baba.
"At this party I can't possibly forget." He smiled at
Ali Baba. "What did you say your nickname was?"

"Ali Baba is not a nickname. I have chosen it
to be my real name. There are too many David
Bernsteins."

"I was the only David Bernstein to finish the New
York City Marathon," said David Bernstein the dentist.
He was the one wearing running shoes.

"The poodles I clip don't care what my name is," said David Bernstein the animal groomer.

"It's not what you're called but what you do that matters," said the seventy-six-year-old David Bernstein.

All of them agreed to that.

"I once read that in some places children are given temporary names. They call them 'milk names.' They can then choose whatever names they want when they get older," said David Bernstein the high-school teacher.

"I'd still choose David Bernstein," said David Bernstein the delicatessen owner. "Just because we all have the same name doesn't make us the same."

"You're right," agreed David Bernstein the mailman.

"Here, here," called out David Bernstein the television director. He raised his glass of apple cider. "A toast to the youngest David Bernstein in the room."

Everyone turned to Ali Baba. He was about to say that he didn't want to be called David. But somehow he didn't mind his name so much now that he had met all these other David Bernsteins. They *were* all different. There would never be another David Bernstein like himself. One of these days he might go back to calling himself David again. But not just now.

"Open your presents," called out David Bernstein the writer.

Even though he had said that they didn't have to, several guests had brought gifts. There was a pocket calculator the size of a business card, just like the one his father had. There was a jigsaw puzzle that looked like a subway map of Manhattan, a model airplane kit, and a few books. One was a collection of Sherlock Holmes stories. "I used to call myself Sherlock Bernstein," the high-school teacher recalled. There was an atlas and, best of all, there was *The Arabian Nights*.

"Now I have my own copy!" said Ali Baba. This was the best birthday he had ever had.

Finally, it was time for the guests to leave. "I never thought I would meet all the David Bernsteins," said David Bernstein the writer.

"You haven't," said Ali Baba. "Besides the seventeen David Bernsteins in the telephone book, there are six hundred eighty-three other Bernsteins listed between Aaron Bernstein and Zachary Bernstein. There must be members of their families who are named David. I bet there are thousands of David Bernsteins that I haven't met yet."

David Bernstein the writer said, "I just might go home and write all about this. When did you get so interested in all the David Bernsteins?"

"It goes back a long time," said Ali Baba. "It all started on the day that I was eight years, five months, and seventeen days old."

◆ LIBRARY LINK ◆

This story was taken from the book The Adventures of Ali Baba Bernstein *by Johanna Hurwitz. You might enjoy reading the entire book to find out if David lives a more exciting life as Ali Baba.*

 Reader's **Response**

Do you agree with the message of this story? Why or why not?

Ali Baba Bernstein

Questions

1. Why didn't David like his name?
2. Where did David find his new name? Why did he choose it?
3. When did Ali Baba first get the idea for his birthday party?
4. How did Ali Baba prepare the invitations for his party? Tell what he did first, second, and so on. Tell how you got your answer.
5. What did Ali Baba find out when he met all the other David Bernsteins?
6. Do you think Ali Baba will keep his new name for his whole life? Why?

Writing to Learn

THINK AND DISCOVER Many people are named David. However, people are different and so are name poems. Read this name poem David might have written.

> Different is what I want to be
> As different as a purple bee
> Very special — that is me
> In every way as you can see!
> Different is what I plan to be.

WRITE Use the first letters of your name and write a name poem. Each line may tell about something you do or like.

55

Just Me

Nobody sees what I can see,
For back of my eyes there is only me.
And nobody knows how my thoughts begin,
For there's only myself inside my skin.

Isn't it strange how everyone owns
Just enough skin to cover his bones?
My father's would be too big to fit—
I'd be all wrinkled inside of it.
And my baby brother's is much too small—
It just wouldn't cover me up at all.
But I feel just right in the skin *I* wear,
And there's nobody like me anywhere.

Margaret Hillert

Vocabulary:

Word Maps

One of the people who came to Ali Baba's party was a *delicatessen* owner. Do you know what a delicatessen is? It fits in this list of words.

> delicatessen
>
> grocery store
>
> supermarket

If you guessed that a delicatessen is a kind of food store, you are correct. Actually, a delicatessen is a food store that sells food that is already cooked.

Words that are alike can be grouped together under one title or category. This is called *classifying.* Classifying words may help you learn their meanings.

Making a Word Map

One way to classify words is to make a word map. A *word map* is a group of words that go with one important or central word. To make a word map, first choose a central word. This is called the *topic.* It should be a word you know. Next, think of words that go with the topic. Last, classify those words so they fit into groups.

Ali Baba Bernstein's guests wore different kinds of clothes to his party. Here is a word map for *clothes.*

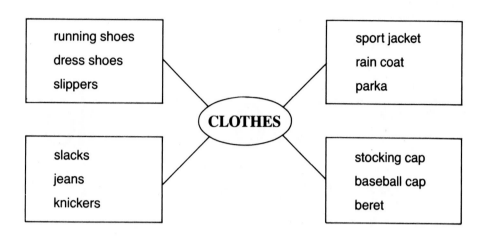

Did you figure out that the categories were kinds of shoes, coats, hats, and pants? Did these categories help you figure out what *parka, knickers,* and *beret* might mean?

Using What You Have Learned

Make a word map with *jobs* as the topic. Think of categories of jobs, and use these words in the map.

dentist	animal groomer	nurse
zoo keeper	high-school teacher	veterinarian
doctor	nursery-school teacher	professor

As You Read

Try to be aware of words that could be grouped together in the next selection, "No Two People Are the Same."

David "Ali Baba" Bernstein wanted to be sure he was different from everyone else. If he were to read this article, he would know that he is!

No Two People Are the Same

by Barbara Branca

Imagine that you and your friend Maria are on your way to her new house. You both get off the school bus and walk up to her front door. Instead of using a key to get into her house, she puts her right eye against the side of the door. She looks into an eye scanner. The scanner looks like a pair of binoculars placed on the wall next to the door. A light studies her eye, and quite suddenly the front door opens wide.

You and Maria go inside and walk down the hall to another door. You hear her shout, "It's Maria!" and the door opens. Maria walks into a room towards a black box on a table. She places her left thumb on the cover of the box, and in a flash it opens. Inside the box is a happy birthday message and a gift.

This sounds unbelievable, doesn't it? But all these things can really happen. The doors and the box that seemed magically to open could tell who Maria was by looking at her eyes and her thumb, and by listening to her voice. How could this be?

Your eyes, voice, and fingertips are one of a kind. That means they are different from everyone else's in the world. Scientists are working to develop computers that use your special characteristics to tell who you are.

Your Fingers Are One of a Kind

Have you ever looked closely at your fingertips? If you do, you will see many tiny lines. Within those lines you will see a circle. Other lines on your fingertips form arches or loops. If you put ink on your fingers and roll them onto paper, you will make fingerprints. Even when you are very old, your fingerprints will still look very much the way they do now.

For thousands of years, people have known that no two people have the same fingerprints. Long, long ago, people used fingerprints instead of signatures as a way of identifying themselves. About a hundred years ago, fingerprinting began to be used as a way to identify people who had committed crimes. Today, we have computers that can identify people by looking at their fingerprints.

Computers that can "read" fingerprints are very special. Information about the shape of the circles, loops, or arches in a fingerprint can be put into the computer's memory. The computer can then identify those patterns when it sees them again. The computer "reads" the finger pattern in the same way that bar codes on food are "read" at a supermarket checkout counter. With the help of these special computers, your fingerprints can act like a secret password that can make doors open and other fantastic things happen.

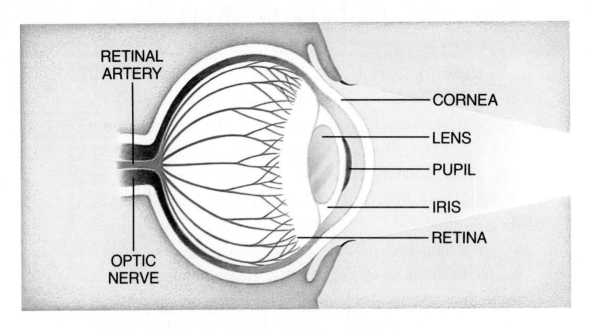

RETINAL ARTERY

CORNEA

LENS

PUPIL

IRIS

RETINA

OPTIC NERVE

Your Eyes Are One of a Kind

You may have known that your fingerprints are one of a kind, but did you know that your eyes are, too? Look in the mirror, and stare into your eyes. In the center of your eye is a dark spot called the pupil. When light enters your eye through the pupil, it hits the back of your eye in a place that you cannot see. That part of your eye is called the retina. It acts like a movie screen. The retina gets pictures of the things that you look at.

Tiny blood vessels crisscross the retina. They make a pattern that looks like a tick-tack-toe board. The chance of someone else having a pattern of blood vessels exactly like yours is a million to one.

Remember when Maria placed her eye on a computer eye scanner at her front door, and the door opened? Well, that scanner read the pattern of blood vessels in Maria's retina and was able to tell who she was. That computer scanner could read the pattern in your eyes, too.

Your Voice Is One of a Kind

Just as no two people have the same eye pattern, no two people sound exactly the same when they talk. Say your name out loud. Then have a friend say your name. Your voices do not sound the same. Some people have high, squeaky voices, while others have soft, quiet ones. Everyone's voice is made up of a pattern of vibrations, or movements. Put your hand on your throat and you will feel the vibrations when you talk.

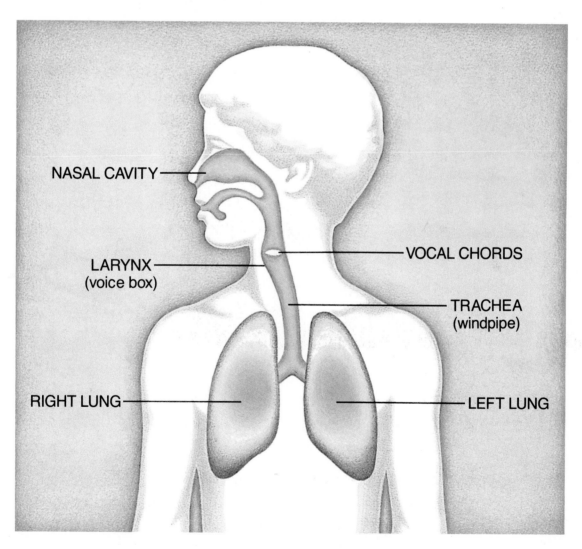

NASAL CAVITY

VOCAL CHORDS

LARYNX
(voice box)

TRACHEA
(windpipe)

RIGHT LUNG

LEFT LUNG

When you speak, air rushes up from your lungs through your throat and into your voice box, at the back of your mouth. Then it travels to the front of your mouth and to your nose. Along this trip, air is forced into many different places. Some places, like your throat, are long and wide. Others, like your nose, are short and narrow. When air goes into a place with a different shape, the sounds you make change. Have you ever noticed how your voice changes when you have a cold? When your nose and throat are swollen, the air from your lungs doesn't have as much room to pass through, and this changes the sound that comes out when you speak.

Some scientists think that there are about fifteen different places inside our bodies that help to shape the sound of our voices. No two people have exactly the same shape in each part. That is why our voices sound so different.

There is a special machine that can draw a picture of the vibrations your voice makes. It is called a sound spectrograph. The sound spectrograph changes the vibrations of your voice into lines that make a picture. The picture it makes is called a voiceprint. If you and your best friend said the same word, your voiceprints would look very different. If you said the same word when you were healthy and then again when you had a cold, your voiceprints would look different from one another. Voiceprints are interesting to look at, and they help to show how each person says words in a different way. However, voiceprints are not useful for telling one person from another because everyone's voice changes from time to time.

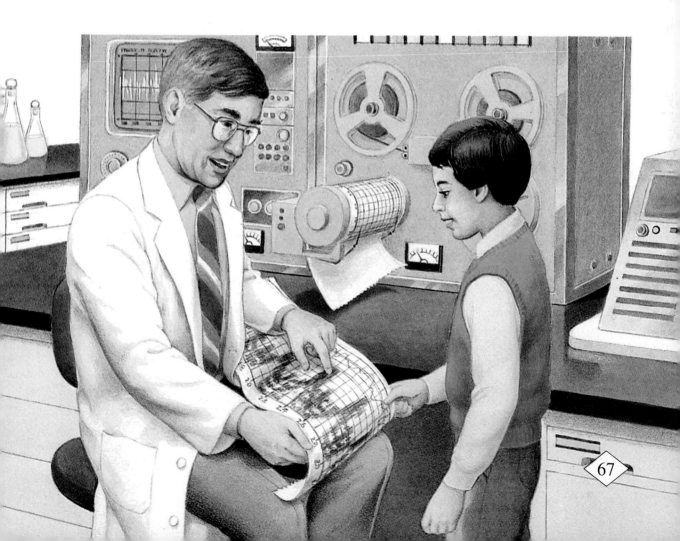

Computers In Your Future

Perhaps in the not-too-distant future, computer scanners will make it possible for people to do all kinds of things, such as taking money from their bank accounts. Work is even being done right now to develop a computer eye scanner to go on cars so that only the owner can open the car door.

Soon, people may be able to buy computers for their homes that can identify only the people who live there. Then you would have no need for a door key, and the only way to get locked out is if you didn't belong there in the first place.

The cost of such computers is very high compared to the cost of a door key. But in the future, as computers become more common, their cost will go down.

Remember Maria at the beginning of the story? She used three computers to get into her house and find her birthday present. Maybe, a few birthdays from now, you will be able to use your fingerprints, voiceprint, or eye pattern to unlock the door to your future.

 Reader's Response

Which of these interesting machines would you most like to try? Explain why.

No Two People Are the Same

 ## Questions

1. Long ago, why did people use fingerprints instead of signatures as a way of identifying themselves?
2. How might using an eye scanner be easier than using a key to open a door? How might it be a problem?
3. Why are fingerprints more useful than voiceprints for identifying a person? Why do you think so?
4. What other tasks might a computer scanner be able to perform?

 ## Writing to Learn

THINK AND INVENT Before you read this article, did you know that each person's eyes, fingerprints, and voice differ? Draw three thumbprints.

WRITE Turn a thumbprint into a creature. Look! Even your drawings of thumbprints are one of a kind! Write an introduction of your thumbprint creature to your classmates.

Building a Nation of Readers

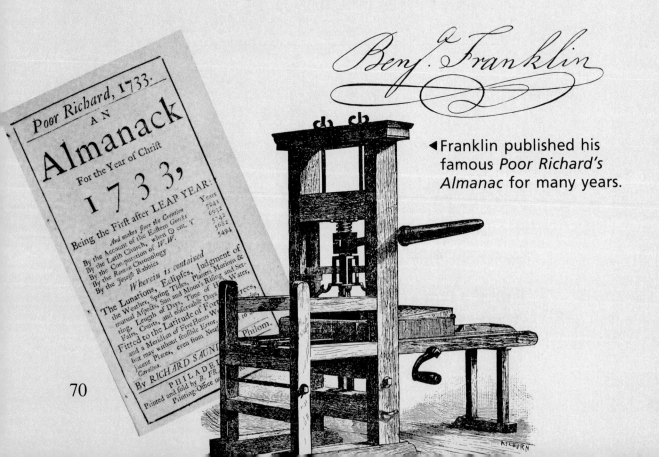

▲ Benjamin Franklin

T hink how you would feel if you went to the library and the librarian said, "I'm sorry but you can't come in here. This library is for members only. The public is not allowed to use it." You'd be surprised because going to a free public library to browse and take out books is so much a part of our lives today.

◄ Franklin published his famous *Poor Richard's Almanac* for many years.

A long time ago in America though, most books were owned by individuals or colleges, and only wealthy people could afford to purchase them. In 1731, Benjamin Franklin helped to set up the first library in the world that made books more widely available to people from all walks of life. Franklin's idea was to gather books in one place so people could borrow them. This idea led to the establishment of free public libraries, which allowed anyone to borrow books and other printed materials. Franklin also gave some of his own books to communities so that they could start their own libraries. This was a powerful idea for a young democratic nation.

Besides starting libraries, Franklin was interested in seeing to it that more people learned how to read. He helped open the Bray Schools in Philadelphia, New York, Williamsburg, and Newport. They were among the very first schools that admitted black children and taught them how to read.

Benjamin Franklin did these things because he knew how important reading was. Today, we still enjoy the world of reading he helped create.

Franklin visits one of the Bray Schools. ▼

Lee Bennett Hopkins
INTERVIEWS

Beverly Cleary

Beverly Bunn Cleary was born in McMinnville, Oregon. Her father was a farmer, her mother a former schoolteacher. She spent the first six years of her life on a farm in Oregon. There, her mother would tell her every story, poem, folk tale, and fairy tale that she could remember.

"Reading meant so much to me as a child," Mrs. Cleary said. "I had read many books about wealthy English children who had nannies or rode in pony carts. *We* knew only about plowhorses! Other books I read were about poor children whose problems were solved by a long-lost, rich relative who turned up in the last chapter.

"I was fortunate to know a teacher-librarian who suggested that I write for children when I grew up. I wanted to read funny stories about the sort of children I knew, and I decided that someday I would write them."

After attending several colleges, Beverly Cleary became a children's librarian in Yakima, Washington. In 1940, she married Clarence Cleary, and they moved to Oakland, California. Upon moving into their new house, she found several piles of typing paper in a linen closet.

"Now I'll have to write a book," she told her husband.

"Why don't you?" he asked.

"Because we never have any sharp pencils," she answered. "The next day my husband went out and brought home a pencil sharpener. I realized that if I was ever going to write a book, this was the time to do it." The result has been the many books that she has created.

The Clearys now live in Carmel, California. They are the parents of grown twins, Marianne and Malcolm. I asked Mrs. Cleary what life was like in a house with a set of twins.

She replied, "Life with twins? It was busy! My novel *Mitch and Amy* came out of their experiences and the experiences of their friends when they were in the fourth grade."

Talking about her writing habits, she said, "Some parts of my stories come out right the first time; others I rewrite several times. A book should be the finished work of an author's imagination. If I start a book and do not like it, I just do not finish it. Writing is a pleasure, and I feel that if I didn't enjoy writing, no one would enjoy reading my books."

While working in Yakima with a group of boys who didn't care about reading, she heard the constant complaint that there weren't any books about "children like us." The boys wanted to read stories that showed the lives of ordinary children.

"Unless you count an essay I wrote about wild animals when I was ten years old, *Henry Huggins* was my first try at writing for children. When I wrote *Henry Huggins*, I wrote for all those little boys in Yakima," she said.

Since *Henry Huggins* appeared in 1950, Beverly Cleary has written close to thirty best-selling books for boys and girls, introducing such wonderful characters as Henry Huggins, Otis Spoford, Beezus, Ellen Tebbits, Ralph S. Mouse, Socks, Leigh Botts, Ramona Quimby and her family—all of whom have become true friends to readers for almost forty years.

Over the years Beverly Cleary has received many awards, including the 1984 Newbery Medal for *Dear Mr. Henshaw*.

The awards she cherishes most, however, are those that are voted on by children from various states. Two such awards she has received are the Mark Twain Award, chosen by children from Missouri, and the Nene Award, chosen by children from Hawaii.

"These awards are most meaningful to me," she says, "because they come from my readers. I am deeply touched that so many girls and boys have voted for my books."

One of the most delightful characters she has created is Ramona Quimby, who first appeared as a minor character in *Henry Huggins*. Over the years, Ramona became a girl readers loved and wanted to know more about. I asked Mrs. Cleary if there was a real Ramona whom she based her character on.

"Not really," she answered, "although emotionally I was like Ramona growing up. I do have my Ramona side *and* my Ellen Tebbits side."

The next story you will read is a selection from *Ramona and Her Father*, a 1978 Newbery Honor Book.

About reading, Beverly Cleary says, "When you read, good things happen. Your life becomes more interesting and so do you. So grab a book. Read all kinds of books, and welcome the world."

Reader's Response

How does the interview show Beverly Cleary's sense of humor?

Beverly Cleary

Questions

1. How were the lives of the children Beverly Cleary read about in books different from her own life?
2. Why do you think reading might have meant so much to her as a child?
3. What happened when Mrs. Cleary and her husband moved into their new home in California?
4. What kinds of children does Mrs. Cleary write about?
5. Why do you think Mrs. Cleary finds awards from children so meaningful? How did you arrive at your answer?

Writing to Learn

THINK AND DECIDE   People become authors for many reasons. Read the "What ifs" below.

> What if a teacher-librarian had not suggested that Mrs. Cleary write books for children?
>
> What if Mrs. Cleary did not move into a new house and find a lot of paper in her linen closet?
>
> What if Mrs. Cleary's husband had not bought her a pencil sharpener?

WRITE   Select one of the "What ifs" and answer it. Tell what you think might have happened.

Ramona's family has a problem, and Ramona can help solve it. All she needs is a million dollars!

Ramona
and the Million Dollars

written by Beverly Cleary
illustrated by Alan Tiegreen

Ramona wished she had a million dollars so her father would be fun again. There had been many changes in the Quimby household since Mr. Quimby had lost his job, but the biggest change was in Mr. Quimby himself.

First of all, Mrs. Quimby found a full-time job working for a doctor, which was good news. However, Mrs. Quimby's new job meant that Mr. Quimby had to be home when Ramona returned from school.

Ramona and her father saw a lot of one
another. At first she thought having her father
to herself for an hour or two every day would be
fun, but when she came home, she found him
running the vacuum cleaner, filling out job
applications, or sitting on the couch staring into
space. He could not take her to the park
because he had to stay near the telephone.
Someone might call to offer him a job. Ramona
grew uneasy. Maybe he was too worried to love
her anymore.

One day Ramona came home to find her
father in the living room staring at the television
set. On the screen a boy a couple of years
younger than Ramona was singing:

Forget your pots, forget your pans.
It's not too late to change your plans.
Spend a little, eat a lot,
Big fat burgers, nice and hot
At your nearest Whopperburger!

Ramona watched him open his mouth wide
to bite into a fat cheeseburger and thought
about the good old days when the family used to
go to the restaurant on payday.

"That kid must be earning a million dollars,"
Mr. Quimby said. "He's singing that commercial
every time I turn on television."

A boy Ramona's age earning a million
dollars? Ramona was all interest. "How's he
earning a million dollars?" she asked.

Mr. Quimby explained. "They make a movie
of him singing the commercial, and every time
the movie is shown on television he gets paid. It
all adds up."

Well! This was a new idea to Ramona.
Singing a song about hamburgers would not be
hard to do. She could do it herself. Maybe she
could earn a million dollars like that boy so her
father would be fun again, and everyone at
school would watch her on television and say,
"There's Ramona Quimby. She goes to our
school."

"Forget your pots, forget your pans," Ramona began to sing.

After that Ramona began to watch for children on television commercials. She saw a boy eating bread and margarine when a crown suddenly appeared on his head with a fanfare—ta *da!*—of music. She saw a girl who took a bite of cereal, giggled, and said, "It's good, hm-um." There was a girl who tipped her head to one side and said, "Pop-pop-pop," as she listened to her cereal. Ramona grew particularly fond of the curly-haired little girl saying to her mother at the zoo, "Look, Mommy, the elephant's legs are wrinkled just like your pantyhose." Ramona could say all those things.

Ramona began to practice. Maybe someone would see her and offer her a million dollars to make a television commercial. On her way to school, she tipped her head to one side and said, "Pop-pop-pop." She said to herself, "M-m-m, it's good," and giggled. Giggling wasn't easy when she didn't have anything to giggle about, but she worked at it.

Since the Quimbys no longer bought potato chips or pickles, Ramona found other foods—toast and apples and carrot sticks—to practice loud crunching on. When they had chicken for dinner, she smacked and licked her fingers.

"Ramona," said Mr. Quimby, "your table manners grow worse and worse. Don't eat so noisily." Ramona was embarrassed. She had been practicing to be on television, and she had forgotten her family could hear.

Ramona continued to practice until she began to feel as if a television camera were watching her wherever she went. She smiled a lot and skipped, feeling that she was cute and lovable. She felt as if she had fluffy blond curls, even though in real life her hair was brown and straight.

One morning, smiling prettily and swinging her lunch box, Ramona skipped to school. Today someone might notice her because she was wearing her red tights. She was happy because this was a special day, the day of Ramona's parent-teacher conference. Since Mrs. Quimby was at work, Mr. Quimby was going to meet with Mrs. Rogers, her third-grade teacher. Ramona was proud to have a father who would come to school.

Feeling dainty, curly-haired, and adorable, Ramona skipped into her classroom, and what did she see but Mrs. Rogers with wrinkles around her ankles. Ramona did not hesitate. She skipped right over to her teacher and, since there did not happen to be an elephant in Room 2, turned the words around and said, "Mrs. Rogers, your pantyhose are wrinkled like an elephant's legs."

Mrs. Rogers looked surprised, and the boys and girls who had already taken their seats giggled. All the teacher said was, "Thank you, Ramona, for telling me. And remember, we do not skip inside the school building."

Ramona had an uneasy feeling she had displeased her teacher.

She was sure of it when her friend Howie said, "Ramona, you sure weren't very polite to Mrs. Rogers." Howie, a serious thinker, was usually right.

Suddenly Ramona was no longer an adorable little fluffy-haired girl on television. She was plain old Ramona, a third-grader whose own red tights bagged at the knee and wrinkled at the ankle. This wasn't the way things turned out on television. On television grown-ups always smiled at everything children said.

That afternoon, when the lower grades had been dismissed from their classrooms, Ramona found her father waiting outside the door of Room 2 for his conference with Mrs. Rogers. Mr. Quimby sat down on a chair outside the door with a folder of Ramona's schoolwork to look over.

Mr. Quimby opened Ramona's folder. "Run along and play on the playground until I'm through," he told his daughter.

Outside, the playground was chilly and damp. Bored, Ramona looked around for something to do, and because she could find nothing better, she followed a traffic guard across the street. On the opposite side, near the market that had been built when she was in kindergarten, she decided she had time to explore. In a weedy space at the side of the market building, she discovered several burdock plants that bore a prickly crop of brown burs, each covered with sharp little hooks.

Ramona saw at once that burs had all sorts of interesting possibilities. She picked two and stuck them together. She added another and another. When she had a string of burs, each clinging to the next, she bent it into a circle and stuck the ends together. A crown! She could make a crown. She picked more burs and built up the circle by making peaks all the way around like the crown the boy wore in the margarine commercial. There was only one thing to do with a crown like that. Ramona crowned herself—ta-*da!*—like the boy on television.

Prickly though it was, Ramona enjoyed
wearing the crown. She practiced looking
surprised, like the boy who ate the margarine.
She pretended she was rich and famous and
about to meet her father, who would be driving
a big shiny car bought with the million dollars
she had earned.

The traffic guards had gone off duty.
Ramona remembered to look both ways before
she crossed the street, and as she crossed she
pretended people were saying, "There goes that
rich girl. She earned a million dollars eating
margarine on TV."

Mr. Quimby was standing on the playground, looking for Ramona. Forgetting all she had been pretending, Ramona ran to him. "What did Mrs. Rogers say about me?" she demanded.

"That's some crown you've got there," Mr. Quimby remarked.

"Daddy, what did she *say?*" Ramona could not contain her impatience.

Mr. Quimby grinned. "She said you were impatient."

Oh, that. People were always telling Ramona not to be so impatient. "What else?" asked Ramona, as she and her father walked toward home.

"You are a good reader, but you are careless about spelling. She said you draw unusually well for a third-grader and your printing is the best in the class."

"What else?"

Mr. Quimby raised one eyebrow as he looked down at Ramona. "She said you were inclined to show off and you sometimes forget your manners."

"I remember my manners most of the time," said Ramona, wondering what her teacher had meant by showing off. Being first to raise her hand when she knew the answer?

"Of course you do," agreed Mr. Quimby. "Now tell me, how are you going to get that crown off?"

Using both hands, Ramona tried to lift her crown but only succeeded in pulling her hair. The tiny hooks clung fast. Ramona tugged. Ow! That hurt. She looked helplessly up at her father.

Mr. Quimby appeared amused. "Who do you think you are? A Rose Festival Queen?"

Ramona pretended to ignore her father's question. How silly to act like someone on television when she was a plain old third-grader. She hoped her father would not guess. He might. He was good at guessing.

By then Ramona and her father were home. As Mr. Quimby unlocked the front door, he said, "We'll have to see what we can do about getting you uncrowned before your mother gets home. Any ideas?"

In the kitchen, Mr. Quimby picked off the top of the crown, the part that did not touch Ramona's hair. That was easy. Now came the hard part.

"Yow!" said Ramona, when her father tried to lift the crown.

"That won't work," said her father. "Let's try one bur at a time." He went to work on one bur, carefully trying to untangle it from Ramona's hair, one strand at a time. To Ramona, who did not like to stand still, this process took forever.

"Yow! Yipe! Leave me some hair," said Ramona, picturing a bald circle around her head.

"I'm trying," said Mr. Quimby and began on the next bur.

After what seemed like a long time, Beezus came home from school. She took one look at Ramona and began to laugh.

"I don't suppose you ever did anything dumb," said Ramona, short of patience and anxious that her sister might guess why she was wearing the remains of a crown. "What about the time you—"

"No arguments," said Mr. Quimby. "We have a problem to solve, and it might be a good idea if we solved it before your mother comes home from work."

Much to Ramona's annoyance, her sister sat down to watch. "How about soaking?" suggested Beezus. "It might soften all those millions of little hooks."

"Yow! Yipe!" said Ramona. "You're pulling too hard."

Mr. Quimby laid another hair-filled bur on the table. "Maybe we should try. This isn't working."

Ramona knelt on a chair with her head in a sinkful of warm water for what seemed like hours until her knees ached and she had a crick in her neck. "Now, Daddy?" she asked at least once a minute.

"Not yet," Mr. Quimby answered, feeling a bur. "Nope," he said at last. "This isn't going to work."

Ramona lifted her dripping head from the sink. When her father tried to dry her hair, the bur hooks clung to the towel. He jerked the towel loose and draped it around Ramona's shoulders.

"Well, live and learn," said Mr. Quimby. "Beezus, scrub some potatoes and throw them in the oven. We can't have your mother come home and find we haven't started supper."

When Mrs. Quimby arrived, she took one look at her husband trying to untangle Ramona's wet hair from the burs, groaned, sank limply onto a kitchen chair, and began to laugh.

By now Ramona was tired, cross, and hungry. "I don't see anything funny," she said sullenly.

Mrs. Quimby managed to stop laughing. "What on earth got into you?" she asked.

Ramona considered. Was this a question grown-ups asked just to be asking a question, or did her mother expect an answer? "Nothing," was a safe reply. She would never tell her family how she happened to be wearing a crown of burs. Never, not even if they threw her into a dungeon.

"Beezus, bring me the scissors," said Mrs. Quimby.

Ramona clapped her hands over the burs. "No!" she shrieked and stamped her foot. "I won't let you cut off my hair!"

Beezus handed her mother the scissors and gave her sister some advice. "Stop yelling. If you go to bed with burs in your hair, you'll really get messed up."

Ramona had to face the wisdom of Beezus's words. She stopped yelling to consider the problem once more. "All right, but I want Daddy to do it."

"I am honored," said Mr. Quimby. "Deeply honored."

Mr. Quimby led Ramona into the living room, where he turned on the television set. "This may take time," he explained, as he went to work. "We might as well watch the news."

Ramona was still anxious. "Don't cut any more than you have to, Daddy," she begged, praying the margarine boy would not appear on the screen. "I don't want everyone at school to make fun of me."

"Just a little," promised her father.

"Does it look awful?" asked Ramona.

"As my grandmother would say, 'It will never be noticed from a trotting horse.'"

Ramona let out a long, shuddery sigh, the closest thing to crying without really crying. *Snip. Snip. Snip.* Ramona touched the side of her head. She still had hair there. More hair than she expected.

The newscaster disappeared from the television screen, and there was that boy again singing:

Forget your pots, forget your pans.
It's not too late to change your plans.

Ramona thought longingly of the days before her father lost his job, when they could forget their pots and pans and change their plans. She watched the boy open his mouth wide and sink his teeth into that fat hamburger with lettuce, tomato, and cheese hanging out of the bun. She swallowed and said, "I bet that boy has a lot of fun with his million dollars." She felt so sad. The Quimbys really needed a million dollars. Even one dollar would help.

Snip. Snip. Snip. "Oh, I don't know," said Mr. Quimby. "Money is handy, but it isn't everything."

"I wish I could earn a million dollars like that boy," said Ramona. This was the closest she would ever come to telling how she happened to set a crown of burs on her head.

"You know something?" said Mr. Quimby. "I don't care how much that kid or any other kid earns. I wouldn't trade you for a million dollars."

"Really, Daddy?" That remark about any other kid—Ramona wondered if her father had guessed her reason for the crown, but she would never ask. Never. "Really? Do you mean it?"

"Really." Mr. Quimby continued his careful snipping. "I'll bet that boy's father wishes he had a little girl who finger-painted and wiped her hands on the cat when she was little and who once cut her own hair so she would be bald like her uncle and who then grew up to be eight years old and crowned herself with burs. Not every father is lucky enough to have a daughter like that."

Ramona giggled. "Daddy, you're being silly!" She was happier than she had been in a long time.

◆ LIBRARY LINK ◆

You can find out what happens to Ramona and her million-dollar dream by reading the rest of the book, Ramona and Her Father *by Beverly Cleary.*

 ## Reader's Response

Would you like to have Ramona Quimby as a friend? What do you like about her? What things might you not like about her?

Writing a Description

In this unit you read about people who are "one of a kind." Which story character did you most admire? Was it Ramona or Ali Baba? Perhaps it was Miss Rumphius. Write sentences that describe the character you chose.

Prewriting

First, draw a picture of your favorite character. Then ask yourself, "How is this person special?" Think about what your character remembers, sees, does, and says. Write your ideas on lines around the picture of the character.

I see birds of paradise.

I remember Grandfather saying, "Make the world more beautiful."

I want to make the world more beautiful.

I planted flower seeds.

I have taken walks through jungles, across deserts, and into libraries.

Writing

Use your notes and picture to write five sentences that describe the character. Write each sentence as if your character were talking. Begin each sentence with *I*. For example, you might write, "I love brightly colored flowers." Be sure your character tells how he or she is one of a kind.

Revising

Read your sentences to yourself. Has your character told why he or she is special? Mark places where you need to add words to make your description clearer.

Proofreading

Use a dictionary to check your spelling. Have you started each sentence with a capital letter? Have you put punctuation marks at the end of each sentence?

Publishing

To play the "One-of-a-Kind Game," copy each sentence onto an index card. Read your sentences, one at a time, to the class. See how many sentences you have to read before your classmates can identify your character.

Making a "One-of-a-Kind" Certificate of Appreciation

In this unit you read about characters who were "one-of-a-kind." Your group will create a certificate of appreciation for one of those story characters in the unit. For example, David Bernstein's certificate might look like the one below. As you work on the certificate, take responsibility for one of the following jobs:

Certificate of Appreciation for David ('Ali Baba') Bernstein

for being one-of-a-kind and learning that what really matters is what you do, not what your name is.

◆ Giving everyone a chance to make suggestions

◆ Writing down everyone's ideas

◆ Reminding the group to keep working

◆ Explaining why your group decided to give the story character a certificate

Together, discuss the story characters in this unit and the reasons why each might deserve a certificate of appreciation. Then choose one story character to receive your certificate.

Talk together about what the certificate might look like and what it might say. Then work together to make a certificate for the character. When you are finished, share your certificate with other people in your class.

BOOKS TO ENJOY

Any Me I Want to Be by Karla Kuskin *(Harper & Row, 1972)* This collection of thirty poems is funny and fun to read. Is the ''me you want to be'' a mirror or the moon?

Did You Carry the Flag Today, Charley? by Rebecca Caudill *(Holt, Rinehart & Winston, 1966)* At Charley's school, carrying the flag is an honor. Charley has never carried the flag, but a surprise is waiting for him!

Ramona the Brave by Beverly Cleary *(Morrow, 1975)* Ramona has a new teacher who doesn't quite know what to make of her. When Ramona meets up with a very large dog, Ramona the Pest becomes Ramona the Brave!

Louis Braille by Margaret Davidson *(Holiday House, 1972)* This biography explains how Louis Braille invented the system of raised dots that permits blind people to read.

GATHER
'ROUND

*S*tories are
fun to read,
fun to hear,
and fun to tell.

*What is a
good story
that you know?*

detail of JUNGLE TALES
(CONTES DE LA JUNGLE),
*oil on canvas by James Jebusa Shannon,
American, 1895*

A STORY A STORY

written and illustrated by Gail E. Haley

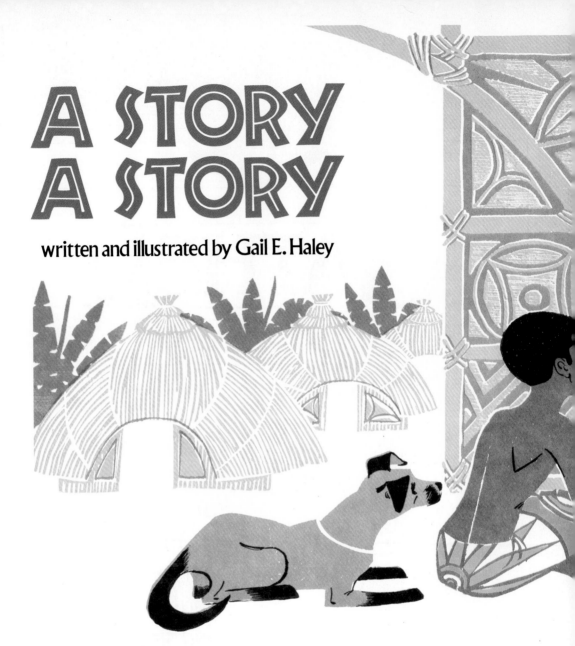

Ananse, the spider man, knows where stories come from. Perhaps he will share his secrets with you.

Many African stories, whether or not they are about Kwaku Ananse (kwä'kyōo u nun se') the "spider man," are called "Spider Stories." This book is about how that came to be.

"Spider Stories" tell how small, defenseless
men or animals outwit others and succeed against
great odds. These stories crossed the Atlantic
Ocean in the cruel ships that delivered slaves to
the Americas. Their descendants still tell some of
these stories today. Ananse has become Anancy
in the Caribbean isles, while he survives as "Aunt
Nancy" in the southern United States.

You will find many African words in this story. If you listen carefully, you can tell what they mean by their sounds. At times words and phrases are repeated several times. Africans repeat words to make them stronger. For example: "So small, so small, so small," means very, very, very small.

The African storyteller begins:

"We do not really mean, we do not really mean that what we are about to say is true. A story, a story; let it come, let it go."

Once, oh small children round my knee, there were no stories on earth to hear. All the stories belonged to Nyame (nyä'mä), the Sky God. He kept them in a golden box next to his royal stool.

Ananse, the spider man, wanted to buy the Sky God's stories. So he spun a web up to the sky.

When the Sky God heard what Ananse wanted, he laughed: "Twe, twe, twe. The price of my stories is that you bring me Osebo the leopard-of-the-terrible-teeth, Mmboro the hornet-who-stings-like-fire, and Mmoatia the fairy-whom-men-never-see."

Ananse bowed and answered: "I shall gladly pay the price."

"Twe, twe, twe," chuckled the Sky God. "How can a weak old man like you, so small, so small, so small, pay my price?"

But Ananse merely climbed down to earth to find the things that the Sky God demanded.

Ananse ran along the jungle path—yiridi, yiridi, yiridi—till he came to Osebo the leopard-of-the-terrible-teeth.

"Oho, Ananse," said the leopard, "you are just in time to be my lunch."

Ananse replied: "As for that, what will happen will happen. But first let us play the binding binding game."

The leopard, who was fond of games, asked: "How is it played?"

"With vine creepers," explained Ananse. "I will bind you by your foot and foot. Then I will untie you, and you can tie me up."

"Very well," growled the leopard, who planned to eat Ananse as soon as it was his turn to bind him.

So Ananse tied the leopard by his foot, by his foot, by his foot, by his foot, with the vine creeper. Then he said: "Now, Osebo, you are ready to meet the Sky God." And he hung the tied leopard in a tree in the jungle.

Next Ananse cut a frond from a banana tree and filled a calabash with water. He crept through the tall grasses, sora, sora, sora, till he came to the nest of Mmboro, the hornets-who-sting-like-fire.

Ananse held the banana leaf over his head as an umbrella. Then he poured some of the water in the calabash over his head.

The rest he emptied over the hornet's nest and cried: "It is raining, raining, raining. Should you not fly into my calabash, so that the rain will not tatter your wings?"

"Thank you. Thank you," hummed the hornets, and they flew into the calabash—fom! Ananse quickly stopped the mouth of the gourd.

"Now, Mmboro, you are ready to meet the Sky God," said Ananse. And he hung the calabash full of hornets onto the tree next to the leopard.

Ananse now carved a little wooden doll holding a bowl. He covered the doll from top to bottom with sticky latex gum. Then he filled the doll's bowl with pounded yams.

He set the little doll at the foot of a flamboyant tree where fairies like to dance. Ananse tied one end of a vine round the doll's head and, holding the other end in his hand, he hid behind a bush.

In a little while, Mmoatia the fairy-whom-men-never-see came dancing, dancing, dancing, to the foot of the flamboyant tree. There she saw the doll holding the bowl of yams.

Mmoatia said: "Gum baby, I am hungry. May I eat some of your yams?"

Ananse pulled at the vine in his hiding place, so that the doll seemed to nod its head. So the fairy took the bowl from the doll and ate all the yams.

"Thank you, Gum baby," said the fairy. But the doll did not answer.

"Don't you reply when I thank you?" cried the angered fairy. The doll did not stir.

"Gum baby, I'll push your crying place unless you answer me," shouted the fairy. But the wooden doll remained still and silent. So the fairy pushed her crying place—pa! Her hand stuck fast to the gum baby's sticky cheek.

"Let go of my hand, or I'll push you again." —Pa! She pushed the doll's crying place with her other hand. Now the fairy was stuck to the gum baby with both hands, and she was furious. She pushed against the doll with her feet, and they also stuck fast.

Now Ananse came out of hiding. "You are ready to meet the Sky God, Mmoatia." And he carried her to the tree where the leopard and the hornets were waiting.

Ananse spun a web round Osebo, Mmboro, and Mmoatia. Then he spun a web to the sky. He pulled up his captives behind him, and set them down at the feet of the Sky God.

"O, Nyame," said Ananse, bowing low, "here is the price you ask for your stories: Osebo the leopard-of-the-terrible-teeth, Mmboro the hornets-who-sting-like-fire, and Mmoatia the fairy-whom-men-never-see."

Nyame the Sky God called together all the nobles of his court and addressed them in a loud voice: "Little Ananse, the spider man, has paid me the price I ask for my stories. Sing his praise. I command you."

"From this day and going on forever," proclaimed the Sky God, "my stories belong to Ananse and shall be called 'Spider Stories.'"

"Eeeee, Eeeee, Eeeee," shouted all the assembled nobles.

So Ananse took the golden box of stories back to earth, to the people of his village. And when he opened the box all the stories scattered to the corners of the world, including this one.

This is my story which I have related. If it be sweet, or if it be not sweet, take some elsewhere, and let some come back to me.

◆ LIBRARY LINK ◆

You can read other stories about Ananse in Oh, Kojo! How Could You! *by Verna Aardema.*

Reader's Response

Would you have treated the animals the same way Ananse did? Why or why not?

A STORY, A STORY

 ## Questions

1. Why did Ananse first go to see Nyame?
2. What did Nyame tell Ananse to do?
3. Why do you think Nyame's price was so high? Explain how you decided on your answer.
4. How was a man as tiny as Ananse able to do what Nyame demanded?
5. What would have happened if Ananse had not been successful?

 ## Writing to Learn

THINK AND IMAGINE What do you think the fairy-whom-men-never-see looks like? Draw a picture, but show only a tiny part of the creature. No one has ever seen all of her.

WRITE Look at your picture. Write why you would or would not like to see this creature in your schoolyard.

A Strategy for Thinking:

Making a Topic Map

How can you decide whether an author is sticking to the point? One way is to make a topic map of each part of an article. Then you can look at your map to see if all the ideas under a topic belong together.

Learning the Strategy

In the article, "No Two People Are the Same," the author wrote about fingerprints. The topic map below was made after reading that part of the article. Look at it, and decide whether all of the facts fit the topic of fingerprints.

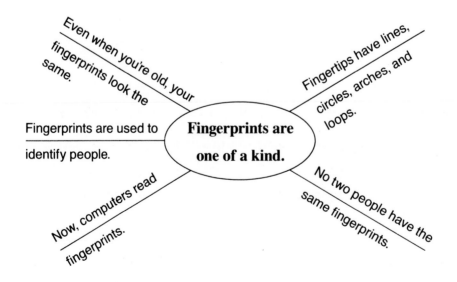

A topic map can look like a bicycle wheel. The topic is written inside a circle at the center of the map. Details and ideas are written on lines that extend out from the circle, like spokes of a wheel.

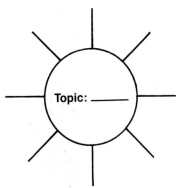

In the map on page 112, all the ideas fit the topic of fingerprints. When all the ideas fit the topic, we can say the author is sticking to the point.

Using the Strategy

Read the section on pages 65−67 about how your voice is one of a kind. On your paper, make a topic map for this section. Then decide whether all the ideas fit the topic. Did the author stick to the point?

Applying the Strategy to the Next Selection

As you read the next article, "The Traveling Storyteller," you will be asked to make a topic map for sections of the article. You can then decide if the author sticks to the point.

◄◆► The writing connection can be found on page 137.

This story is about a teller of stories.
Meet Linda Goss!

The Traveling Storyteller

by Linda Goss

114

Storytelling is an art form that brings people together. All over the world, people love to listen to stories. I love to tell stories. My name is Linda Goss. I am a traveling storyteller.

I was born near the Great Smoky Mountains in Alcoa, Tennessee. All the members of my family loved stories, so I grew up with storytelling. My mother told me stories from the Bible. My favorite one was about a man named Jonah, who was swallowed by a whale. My father told me funny versions of popular fairy tales, such as Cinderella.

Perhaps my grandfather's stories had the greatest influence on me. I called my grandfather "Grand-daddy Murphy." He told me all kinds of stories, especially tales of his childhood and folk tales he remembered hearing when he was a boy. Grand-daddy Murphy's favorite folk tales were about "Brer Rabbit." Brer Rabbit was a clever animal who often played tricks on Brer Bear and Brer Fox. "But sometimes Brer Rabbit's cleverness got the best of him," Grand-daddy Murphy would say as he ended a story. I would laugh and he would tell me another one.

I have forgotten some of the stories my family told me. The ones I do remember I have passed down to my daughters, Aisha and Uhuru, and my son, Jamaal. I hope they will pass down the stories to their children, and so on, and so on.

◄ **Linda Goss gets ready to tell a story.**

How I Became a Professional Storyteller

I have always kept the love for storytelling deep inside me. So, I decided to become a professional storyteller and share my stories with the world. A professional storyteller is a person who earns a living by telling stories. I became a professional storyteller in Washington, D.C., in 1973. At that time, my husband, Clay Goss, was teaching at Howard University. One day he came home from work and said, "Linda, the university is looking for a storyteller." I answered, "Well, here I am!"

Make a topic map for this section.

116

I was used to telling stories to my children at home, but not to strangers. Would I be able to do it? Then the moment came when I was on stage. I looked at the audience. They were all looking at me. I was very nervous. I was scared, too. But as I thought about the stories, I forgot how scared and nervous I was. When I finished, the audience clapped. They said that they liked the way I told stories. Suddenly, they no longer seemed like strangers to me. From that day on I knew I would always tell stories.

While I was in Washington, D.C., I was invited to tell stories at the Martin Luther King, Jr. Library, the Smithsonian Institution, and even at President's Park on the White House lawn. Then my family and I moved from Washington, D.C., to Philadelphia, Pennsylvania. No one there knew I was a professional storyteller, so I decided to return to teaching.

I told stories to my students every day. Before long, their parents wanted me to tell them stories at workshops and churches. Other teachers in the school wanted me to tell them stories in workshops, too. Soon, other schools were inviting me to come and tell stories.

◀ **Linda Goss is telling an Ananse story to a group of students at a school in Philadelphia, Pennsylvania.**

Some people who liked my stories formed a group called "Friends of Linda Goss." They invited me to tell stories at a library in Germantown, a neighborhood in Philadelphia. Five hundred people came to hear me. The next thing I knew, I was telling stories everywhere. I traveled on airplanes, trains, and riverboats to get to places where I had been invited to tell stories. I had become a traveling storyteller. ❖

❖

Did all the ideas fit the topic?

Where I Find Stories

I find stories in many different places and get them in many different ways. I get them from books, friends, other storytellers, and from countries around the world. Some of the stories I tell are folk tales. These are stories that have been passed down from one generation to the next. Folk tales were first told aloud. They were not written down for many, many years. Some of the folk tales I enjoy telling are "how and why" tales. A "how and why" tale tries to explain how or why something came to be. For example, it may tell how the elephant got its long trunk, or why bears have short tails. I also make up some of my stories, and sometimes, my husband writes stories for me. ❖

❖

Make a topic map for this section.

My favorite stories come from Ghana, a country in West Africa. That is where Ananse the Spider is supposed to have come from. I have been telling Ananse stories for over ten years. Some people say that Ananse was the first storyteller. There are thousands of stories about him, like the one you read in this book.

Did the author stick to the point?

How I Tell Stories

I try to make my storytelling programs exciting and special. I always begin by ringing large bells. Then I chant, "Story, storytelling time." This lets the audience know that it is time to listen. I wear brightly colored gowns. Most of these gowns are made out of cloths from Africa. They have drawings on them of birds, fish, butterflies, and yes, even Ananse the Spider.

Make a topic map for this section.

Linda Goss uses cloth from Africa to make her storytelling gowns. ▶

119

When I tell Ananse stories, I try to move my arms and fingers as Ananse might have. I try to show different expressions on my face, as Ananse might have.

I carry a "goodie bag" full of cloths when I tell stories. These cloths come from many different countries. I use the cloths to help tell stories. One cloth might become the wind, another a rain forest. I even carry an Ananse cloth in my goodie bag.

The audience also helps me tell stories. They help me create a special place by moving their arms and making sounds that animals make. They move around and sing, and pretend to become the animal characters in the stories. The audience and I have a wonderful time together. To me, that is what storytelling is all about. ◆◆◆

Did making topic maps help you understand the organization of this article? How?

◆ LIBRARY LINK ◆

You may not be able to hear Linda Goss tell her stories, but you can read ones like them yourself. Try Tales of an Ashanti Father, *retold by Peggy Appiah.*

Reader's Response

Would you like to hear Linda Goss tell one of her stories? How might listening to her tell the story be different from reading it yourself?

The Traveling Storyteller

Questions

1. When did Linda Goss first begin to enjoy storytelling?
2. What were some of the first stories she heard?
3. Why is Linda Goss called a "traveling storyteller"?
4. Tell three ways in which Linda Goss makes her stories exciting for the audience. Describe how you decided on your answer.
5. How do you think Linda Goss prepares to tell a story? List some things she might do.

Writing to Learn

THINK AND PLAN   Be a storyteller. Add to this list of things a storyteller can do to make a "telling" interesting.

How to Tell Stories
- Get attention! Ring a bell.
- Show expression on your face.
-
-
-

WRITE   Name a story that you would like to tell to your classmates. Write two reasons why your classmates might enjoy the story you chose.

*Mrs. Maeberry can't wait to tell her children
some surprising news. However, she gets an even
bigger surprise herself!*

Nothing Much Happened Today

by Mary Blount Christian

Mrs. Maeberry held her groceries tightly.
She scurried home to tell her children about
seeing the police chase a robber. But when she
turned down her sidewalk, her mouth flew open.
Soap bubbles—hundreds, thousands, maybe
millions of soap bubbles—were drifting from her
front window. She ran inside. "What's
happened?" she demanded. "What's happened
here?"

Stephen shrugged. "Nothing much, really."

"But the bubbles!" she yelled. "Look at
those bubbles!"

Stephen shrugged again.

Elizabeth mumbled, "I guess maybe we did use too many suds when we bathed Rusty."

"The dog? You bathed the dog?" Mother screamed. "Why did you bathe the dog?"

"He got sugar stuck all over his fur," Alan, the youngest, said.

Mother set her groceries down. "I was gone five minutes. How could Rusty get sugar in his fur?"

"He got sugar in his fur when he knocked over the sugar sack. That was when he was chasing the cat through the kitchen," Stephen added.

Mother gasped. "Cat? Cat? We don't *have* a cat."

"I guess you could say it was a visiting cat," Stephen explained. "It came through the window."

"The window?" Mother shrieked. "That cat broke the glass?"

Stephen shook his head. "Nope. The window was open. We had to let the smoke out."

Mother grabbed her forehead. "Smoke! What smoke?"

"The smoke from the oven when the cake batter spilled over," Elizabeth volunteered.

Mother waved her arms. "Why were you baking a cake?"

"For the school bake sale," Alan reminded her.

"But," Mother protested. "But I baked that before I went to the store."

"We know," Stephen said, "but that one got ruined."

"Ruined?" Mother repeated. "How could my beautiful cake get ruined? I was gone ten minutes, only ten minutes."

"The cake was knocked onto the floor, and it's a good thing it was, too," Elizabeth said.

"I don't understand this. I don't understand this at all," Mother said.

"It's not so bad," Stephen said. "We used too many soap suds on Rusty because he was covered with sugar. He knocked the sugar over chasing the cat. The cat came through the window when we let out the smoke. The smoke is from the spilled cake batter in the oven. We were replacing the cake you baked because that one got knocked off by the police officer."

Mother's eyebrows shot up. "Police officer! What police officer?"

"The police officer that ran in after the robber," Alan told her.

"MY robber?" Mother gasped. "I—I mean the grocery robber?" She sank into a chair. "But tell me, please. Tell me how a robber and a police officer ruined my cake."

Stephen smiled. "That's easy. The robber ran around and around our kitchen table. The police officer went around and around after him. The police officer accidentally knocked the cake to the floor. The robber skidded in the icing."

Elizabeth interrupted. "And when the robber fell, he hit his head on Alan's head. And you know how hard Alan's head is."

127

"I know. I know," Mother said. "Let me see now. The robber ran in here and the police officer chased him. They ruined the cake. When you baked a new one you made the oven smoky. Then you opened the window to let the smoke out and the cat came in. Rusty chased the cat and knocked the sack of sugar on himself. And that's when you bathed him with too many suds?"

"That's right," the three children said together. "And that's when you came home."

"Twenty minutes at the most," Mother said. "I *know* I couldn't have been gone more than twenty minutes, anyway."

"We *told* you nothing much happened today," Stephen said. "How was your day?"

"Nothing much," Mother said, sliding further back into the chair. "Nothing much." The last soap bubble floated gently to the end of her nose where it rested, then popped, and was gone.

 Reader's Response

Which part of this story do you think would make the funniest cartoon?

Nothing Much Happened Today

Questions

1. Why was Mrs. Maeberry in such a hurry to get home?
2. Why do you think the children told their mother that nothing much happened while she was shopping?
3. What happened when the children opened the window?
4. How would you describe Mrs. Maeberry's reaction to what her children told her? What clues told you this?
5. List several ways the children tried to fix things before their mother got home.

Writing to Learn

THINK AND CONNECT   In "Nothing Much Happened Today," one thing leads to another. Copy the "thought link" below. Fill in the second link.

Because the policeman chased the robber into the house,

they ruined the cake.

When they baked a new cake,

WRITE   Make up your own "thought link" about a funny experience you remember. In the first link write "Because ___," and in the second link write what happened next. Finish the links with your own words.

129

King Midas
and the Golden Touch

Retold by
Judy Rosenbaum

Sometimes, when a wish comes true, the results can surprise you.

Once upon a time there was a very rich king named Midas. He lived in a fine castle with his daughter, Marygold. The two things he loved best in life were gold and Marygold. He loved to go into his treasure room and count his coins. No one, not even Marygold, was allowed into the king's treasure room.

One day Midas was sitting in the treasure
room dreaming about his gold. In his dream, he
saw a shadow fall across the piles of valuable gold
coins. He looked up and saw a stranger standing
near him. Since no one was allowed into his
treasure room, Midas was surprised. The stranger
looked kind, however, so Midas wasn't afraid. He
greeted the man, and they began to talk of gold.

"You certainly have a lot of gold," said the
stranger.

"It's not so much," said Midas.

The stranger smiled. "Do you want even
more gold than this?" he asked.

"If I had my way, everything I touched would
turn into gold," Midas replied.

The stranger's smile grew wider. "So you
want the Golden Touch? Very well, I will give it
to you. At sunrise tomorrow, you will be able to
turn anything you touch into gold."

Midas was so excited that he could hardly wait until morning. At last the sun rose. Still dreaming, Midas sat up and reached for the water jug by his bed. At once it became gold. Midas was so overjoyed, he got up and danced around the room, touching everything within his reach. Soon, he had a room full of gleaming gold objects. When he reached for his clothes, they turned into heavy golden cloth. "Now I shall really look like a king," he said. He got dressed and admired himself in the mirror. Midas was impressed by his golden clothes, though they were so heavy he could hardly move.

His looking glass was more of a problem. He tried to use it to see his new treasures better. To his surprise, he could not see anything through it. He put it on the table and found that it was now gold, but Midas was too excited to worry. He said, "I can see well enough without it. Besides, it is much more valuable now."

Midas went down to his rose garden. There, he touched rosebush after rosebush. Soon, one whole corner of the garden was filled with golden roses. Their bright petals reflected the sun, and their stems had become thin gold wires. Even the thorns on the rosebushes had turned into gold. Midas was completely happy.

After some time had passed, Midas realized that he was hungry. He went into the dining room to get his breakfast. There was bread, milk, and a tasty cooked fish on the table. Two places had been set, one for Midas and one for Marygold. Midas sat down and waited for his little daughter. He was eager to show her his new power.

When Marygold arrived, Midas was surprised to see that she was crying. "Why are you sad on such a wonderful morning?" he asked.

Marygold held up a golden rose. "Look at what has happened to the flowers in our lovely garden," she said. "Our roses have no smell anymore. Their petals have become hard, with sharp edges, and they have such an ugly color!"

Midas was too ashamed to tell Marygold how the roses had become hard and golden. So he just said, "Now, now, Marygold, everything will be all right."

Marygold sat down, but she didn't cheer up. She was so upset that she didn't notice what was going on at the table. Midas was having a lot of trouble with his breakfast. When he took a piece of bread, it turned into a golden lump in his hand. The fish became a beautiful, but useless, golden fish with tiny gold bones. The milk in his cup hardened into metal when his lips touched it. "If this goes on, I'll never be able to eat again," said poor Midas.

Marygold looked up. "Father, what's wrong?" she asked. Then she saw all the shining food on the gleaming dishes in front of her father. "Oh, poor Father," she said. She gave him some of her food, but it too turned into gold. Marygold felt terrible for her father. She hurried over to comfort him. As she threw her arms around him, Midas let out a warning cry, but it was too late. His daughter had turned into a silent golden statue. Even the tears on her cheeks had turned into tiny drops of gold. "Oh, what a terrible thing I have done!" cried Midas.

Midas, with great sadness, sat next to poor Marygold for a long time. After a while, he heard someone in the doorway. He looked up. There stood the stranger in his dream. "I see the Golden Touch has not made you happy," the stranger said gently.

"I would do anything to get rid of this terrible gift," Midas said.

The stranger said, "Go and wash yourself in the river. Then splash water from the river on everything that you turned into gold."

Midas thanked the stranger, grabbed a huge jug, and rushed outside. When he ran through the garden, more roses turned to gold as he brushed past them. Midas reached the river and walked in. He stayed there for a long time before getting out. Then he nervously touched a flower growing along the river. It did not change to gold. "I'm cured!" Midas shouted. He picked up his gold jug and filled it with water. At once it became an ordinary jug again. Midas ran with the jug to Marygold. As soon as he poured the water on his beloved daughter, her skin became soft, and she began to move. Midas hugged her joyfully.

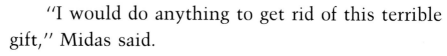

Midas and Marygold went through the house and the garden. They splashed water from the river on everything Midas had turned into gold. They didn't leave out even one rose.

After what seemed like a very long time, Midas woke up. He realized that everything that he thought had happened was only a dream. Midas' dream had taught him an important lesson. His love for his daughter was more important than all the gold in the world.

Many, many years later, when Midas was a grandfather, he would hold Marygold's children on his knees and tell them about his dream, very much the way I've told it to you. When he finished, he would stroke the children's golden curls. Then he would tell them that the gold in their hair was the only gold he valued.

Reader's Response

Have you ever had a wish come true, only to be disappointed? Explain.

King Midas
and the Golden Touch

 ## Questions

1. What was King Midas's greatest wish?
2. When did the king begin to see that the Golden Touch was a problem?
3. What did King Midas learn after he turned his daughter into gold?
4. Why do you think the stranger came back the second time? What reasons led you to your opinion?
5. If you could change one thing about this story, what would it be?

 ## Writing to Learn

THINK AND ORGANIZE   A semantic map will help you see the effects of the golden touch. Make a semantic map on your paper like this one, and complete it.

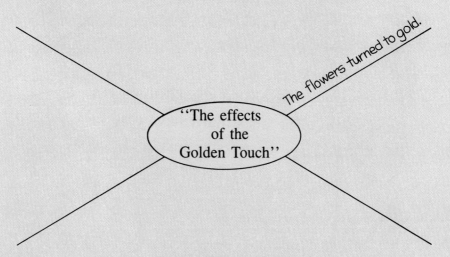

WRITE   Write about the effects of the Golden Touch. Use the semantic map to organize your thoughts.

I'll Tell You a Story

I'll tell you a story
About Jack a Nory,
And now my story's begun;

I'll tell you another
Of Jack and his brother,
And now my story is done.

Mother Goose

Reading

A story is a special thing.
The ones that I have read,
They do not stay inside the books.
They stay inside my head.

Marchette Chute

There was an old pig with a pen
Who wrote stories and verse now and then.
To enhance these creations,
He drew illustrations
With brushes, some paints and his pen.

written and illustrated by Arnold Lobel
from The Book of Pigericks

*Sometimes even a great emperor can learn
something from a child.*

The Emperor's Plum Tree

written and illustrated by Michelle Nikly
translated by Elizabeth Shub

140

Long ago,
in the land of the rising sun, there lived an emperor
whose garden was beautiful beyond imagination. Each
tree, each flower, each stone had its place in the total
harmony of the design.

One morning as the emperor took his daily walk, he
stopped in dismay at a grove of plum trees. Could that
tree near the wall be dying? He hurried to it. He felt a
twig. It broke off in his hand, hard and dry. The tree
would have to be cut down. The perfect garden would
be perfect no longer. The emperor shut himself up in
his palace and refused to go out.

Days passed, and indoors, the emperor mourned his garden. At last it was decided that only a plum tree as beautiful as the one that died could bring back the perfect harmony of the garden and make the emperor happy again. Messengers were sent to search the land and within a day a perfect tree was found in the garden of a painter named Ukiyo (oo′ kē yō).

Ukiyo, his wife Tanka (täng′ ku), and their small son Musuko (moo soo′ kō) were saddened when they learned that their tree had been chosen for the imperial garden. Ukiyo loved to paint its twisted branches and starlike flowers, and many of the poems Tanka wrote described its beauty.

 But most of all,
the plum tree was the home of Musuko's friend, the
nightingale. Musuko often stood at the foot of the tree
and spoke to her. She replied in her own way, yet they
always understood one another as true friends do.

Ukiyo knew they had to part with the tree, but he
asked if they might keep it one day longer.

When the plum tree was about to be taken away,
Musuko approached the emperor's messenger. He asked
if he might tie a scroll to one of its branches. The
messenger, seeing how bravely the boy choked back his
tears, lifted him up so that he could attach the scroll.

The plum tree was replanted in the imperial garden and the emperor was persuaded to come and see it. He gazed at it while the messengers waited anxiously. At last, to everyone's relief, he smiled. The emperor's garden was perfect once again.

Then the emperor noticed Musuko's scroll. He took it down and unrolled it.

What he saw was a wonderfully lifelike drawing of a branch of the plum tree, and perched on the branch was a nightingale. Beneath the painting was a poem.

At the long day's end,
when the nightingale flies home,
what shall I tell her?

For a long time, the emperor stood in thought before the plum tree. Then he sent a messenger to bring Ukiyo, Tanka, and Musuko to the palace. The following day, they appeared before him. He spoke first to Musuko.

"My child," the emperor said. "I will tell you what to say to your homeless friend. Tell her that her plum tree, borrowed for a day because of the emperor's whim, will be returned to her by the emperor's order."

Ukiyo and Tanka were about to protest, but the emperor would not let them.

"It seems that my sorrow has been replaced by yours. I could not bear to see this tree each day, knowing that a child lost his friend because of me. This tree belongs in your garden, but before it leaves mine, I have a request. Ukiyo, I ask you to paint my garden, perfect as it is on this day.

"The death of my plum tree has reminded me that no garden can last forever. One day the peach trees, the pines, and even the bamboos will be no more. But your painting, Ukiyo, will be a lasting reminder of this garden's perfection.

"And, Tanka, I ask you to write this story, just as it happened, so that in times to come children will hear how once the Emperor of Japan learned wisdom from a small boy named Musuko, a nightingale, and a plum tree."

Reader's Response

What was appealing to you about this story?

The Emperor's Plum Tree

Questions

1. Why was the emperor unhappy about his plum tree?
2. Why was Musuko unhappy about his plum tree?
3. How did the emperor's feelings change after he read Musuko's scroll? What clues make you think so?
4. What made the emperor return the tree?
5. Do you think the emperor will be unhappy about his garden again? Explain why or why not.

Writing to Learn

THINK AND CREATE Musuko wins the emperor's understanding with a little poem. His poem explains the gentle nightingale's problem.

	Subject	Problem
	a nightingale	may need a home
	a leaf	may need fall's glorious color
	a stone	may need some soft green moss
	a raindrop	may need a sparkle

WRITE Read Musuko's poem. Then write your own little poem. Write about something in nature and a problem it might have.

Literature:

Characterization

You know people you could describe as curious. You could describe other people you know as hard-working or fun-loving or brave or honest or sad. You meet characters in your reading that you might describe in the same ways.

Authors try to make their stories seem real by showing or telling you what the characters are like. The way the author lets you know about a character is called characterization.

Direct Telling by an Author

Sometimes an author simply tells you about a character. In "Ramona and the Million Dollars" the author says:

> One morning, smiling prettily and swinging her lunch box, Ramona skipped to school.

The author is telling us that Ramona is a happy, lively girl.

Conversation of the Characters

At other times you know what a character is like by what he or she says. In "King Midas and the Golden Touch," Midas says:

"If I had my way, everything I touched would turn into gold."

From what King Midas says, you know that he can be greedy, and that he isn't always very thoughtful.

Actions of the Characters

Sometimes the author describes what the character does and lets you decide what this tells you about the character. In "The Emperor's Plum Tree" the emperor discovered a dying tree in his garden. Then the author says:

The emperor shut himself up in his palace and refused to go out.

The author doesn't come right out and say it, but you know that the emperor likes things to be perfect and gets very upset when things go wrong.

In "The Big Orange Splot" the author writes:

When the other people came out of their houses, they saw Mr. Plumbean swinging in a hammock between two palm trees....Mr. Plumbean was drinking lemonade.

What is the author telling us about Mr. Plumbean?

Read and Enjoy

As you read "Sam, Bangs & Moonshine," watch for the way the author uses characterization. Knowing about characterization will help you understand what you read.

150

Sam loves to tell stories, until her "moonshine" gets a friend into big trouble.

Sam, Bangs & Moonshine

written and illustrated by Evaline Ness

On a small island, near a large harbor, there once lived a fisherman's little daughter (named Samantha, but always called Sam), who had the reckless habit of lying.

Not even the sailors home from the sea could tell stranger stories than Sam. Not even the ships in the harbor, with curious cargoes from giraffes to gerbils, claimed more wonders than Sam did.

Sam said her mother was a mermaid, when everyone knew she was dead.

Sam said she had a fierce lion at home, and a baby kangaroo. (Actually, what she *really* had was an old wise cat called Bangs.)

Sam even said that Bangs could talk, if and when he wanted to.

Sam said this. Sam said that. But you could never believe what Sam said.

Even Bangs yawned and shook his head when
she said the ragged old rug on the doorstep was a
chariot drawn by dragons.

Early one morning, before Sam's father left in his fishing boat to be gone all day, he hugged Sam hard and said, "Today, for a change, talk REAL not MOONSHINE. MOONSHINE spells trouble."

Sam promised. But while she washed the dishes, made the beds, and swept the floor, she wondered what he meant. When she asked Bangs to explain REAL and MOONSHINE, Bangs jumped on her shoulder and purred, "MOONSHINE is flummadiddle. REAL is the opposite." Sam decided that Bangs made no sense whatever.

When the sun made a golden star on the cracked window, Sam knew it was time to expect Thomas.

Thomas lived in the tall grand house on the hill. Thomas had two cows in the barn, twenty-five sheep, a bicycle with a basket, and a jungle-gym on the lawn. But most important of all, Thomas believed every word Sam said.

At the same time every day, Thomas rode his bicycle down the hill to Sam's house and begged to see her baby kangaroo.

Every day Sam told Thomas it had just "stepped out." She sent Thomas everywhere to find it. She sent him to the tallest trees where, she said, it was visiting owls. Or perhaps it was up in the old windmill, grinding corn for its evening meal.

"It might be," said Sam, "in the lighthouse tower, warning ships at sea."

"Or maybe," she said, "it's asleep on the sand, somewhere, anywhere on the beach."

Wherever Sam sent Thomas, he went. He climbed up trees, ran down steps, and scoured the beach, but he never found Sam's baby kangaroo.

While Thomas searched, Sam sat in her chariot and was drawn by dragons to faraway secret worlds.

Today, when Thomas arrived, Sam said, "That baby kangaroo just left to visit my mermaid mother. She lives in a cave behind Blue Rock."

Sam watched Thomas race away on his bicycle over the narrow path that stretched to a massive blue rock in the distance. Then she sat down in her chariot. Bangs came out of the house and sat down beside Sam. With his head turned in the direction of the diminishing Thomas, Bangs said, "When the tide comes up, it covers the road to Blue Rock. Tide rises early today."

Sam looked at Bangs for a minute. Then she said, "Pardon me while I go to the moon."

Bangs stood up. He stretched his front legs. Then he stretched his back legs. Slowly he stalked away from Sam toward Blue Rock.

Suddenly Sam had no desire to go to the moon. Or any other place either. She just sat in her chariot and thought about Bangs and Thomas.

She was so busy thinking that she was unaware of thick, muddy clouds that blocked out the sun. Nor did she hear the menacing rumble of thunder. She was almost knocked off the doorstep when a sudden gust of wind drove torrents of rain against her face.

Sam leaped into the house and slammed the door. She went to the window to look at Blue Rock, but she could see nothing through the grey ribbed curtain of rain. She wondered where Thomas was. She wondered where Bangs was. Sam stood there looking at nothing, trying to swallow the lump that rose in her throat.

The murky light in the room deepened to black. Sam was still at the window when her father burst into the house. Water streamed from his hat and oozed from his boots. Sam ran to him screaming, "Bangs and Thomas are out on the rock! Blue Rock! Bangs and Thomas!"

As her father turned quickly and ran out the door, he ordered Sam to stay in the house.

"And pray that the tide hasn't covered the rock!" he yelled.

When her father had gone, Sam sat down. She listened to the rain hammer on the tin roof. Then suddenly it stopped. Sam closed her eyes and mouth, tight. She waited in the quiet room. It seemed to her that she waited forever.

At last she heard her father's footsteps outside. She flung open the door and said one word: "Bangs?"

Sam's father shook his head.

"He was washed away," he said. "But I found Thomas on the rock. I brought him back in the boat. He's home now, safe in bed. Can you tell me how all this happened?"

Sam started to explain, but sobs choked her. She cried so hard that it was a long time before her father understood everything.

Finally, Sam's father said, "Go to bed now. But before you go to sleep, Sam, tell yourself the difference between REAL and MOONSHINE."

Sam went to her room and crept into bed. With her eyes wide open she thought about REAL and MOONSHINE.

MOONSHINE was a mermaid-mother, a fierce lion, a chariot drawn by dragons, and certainly a baby kangaroo. It was all flummadiddle just as Bangs had told her. Or *had* he told her? Wouldn't her father say that a cat's talking was MOONSHINE?

REAL was no mother at all. REAL was her father and Bangs. And now there wasn't even Bangs. Tears welled up in Sam's eyes again. They ran down into her ears making a scratching noise. Sam sat up and blew her nose. The scratching was not in her ears. It was at the window. As Sam stared at the window, two enormous yellow eyes appeared and stared back. Sam sprang from her bed and opened the window. There sat Bangs, his coat a sodden mess.

"Oh, Bangs!" cried Sam, as she grabbed and smothered him with kisses. "What happened to you?"

In a few words Bangs told her that one moment he was on the rock with Thomas and the next he was lying at the foot of the lighthouse tower a mile away. Strong waves had pushed him there.

"Nasty stuff, water," Bangs grumbled, as he washed himself from his ears to his feet.

Sam patted Bangs. "Well, at least it's not flummadiddle. . . ." Sam paused. She looked up to see her father standing in the doorway.

"Look! Bangs is home!" shouted Sam.

"Hello, Bangs. What's not flummadiddle?" asked Sam's father.

"Bangs! And you! And Thomas!" answered Sam. "Oh, Daddy! I'll always know the difference between REAL and MOONSHINE now. Bangs and Thomas were almost lost because of MOONSHINE. Bangs told me."

"He *told* you?" questioned Sam's father.

"Well, he would have *if* he could talk," said Sam. Then she added sadly, "I know cats can't talk like people, but I almost believed I *did* have a baby kangaroo."

Her father looked steadily at her.

"There's good MOONSHINE and bad MOON-SHINE," he said. "The important thing is to know the difference." He kissed Sam good night and left the room.

When he had closed the door, Sam said, "You know, Bangs, I might just keep my chariot."

This time Bangs did not yawn and shake his head. Instead he licked her hand. He waited until she got into bed, then he curled up at her feet and went to sleep.

The next morning Sam opened her eyes to see an incredible thing! Hopping toward her on its hind legs was a small, elegant, large-eyed animal with a long tail like a lion's. Behind it strolled Bangs and her father.

"A baby kangaroo!" shouted Sam. "Where did you find it!"

"It is *not* a baby kangaroo," said Sam's father. "It's a gerbil. I found it on an African banana boat in the harbor."

"Now Thomas can see a baby kangaroo at last!" Sam squealed with joy.

Sam's father interrupted her. "Stop the MOONSHINE, Sam. Call it by its REAL name. Anyway, Thomas won't come today. He's sick in bed with laryngitis. He can't even talk. Also his bicycle got lost in the storm."

Sam looked down at the gerbil. Gently she stroked its tiny head. Without raising her eyes, she said, "Daddy, do you think I should *give* the gerbil to Thomas?"

Sam's father said nothing. Bangs licked his tail.

Suddenly Sam hollered, "Come on, Bangs!"

She jumped out of bed and slipped into her shoes. As she grabbed her coat, she picked up the gerbil, and ran from the house with Bangs at her heels. Sam did not stop running until she stood at the side of Thomas's bed.

Very carefully she placed the gerbil on Thomas's stomach. The little animal sat straight up on its long hind legs and gazed directly at Thomas with its immense round eyes.

"Whaaaaaaaaaaa sis name!" wheezed Thomas.

"MOONSHINE," answered Sam, as she gave Bangs a big wide smile.

 Reader's Response

Would you like to have Sam for a friend? Tell why or why not.

Writing a Folk Tale

Do you know how the tiger got its stripes? In one folk tale, while the yellow tiger was sleeping, his friends Hyena and Jackal painted stripes on him as a joke. When the tiger awoke, the paint had dried and the stripes have been there ever since.

Folk tales, like the tale of the tiger and his stripes, are stories that often explain how or why things came to be. For example, there are folk tales that tell where the oceans came from or why rabbits have long ears.

Use your imagination to write a tale that explains how something began or where something came from.

Prewriting

Choose a question of your own. Here are some ideas that may help you think of a good topic for your story.

♦ Where do rainbows come from?

♦ What makes the sky blue?

♦ Why does an elephant have a long trunk?

On your paper, draw a diagram like the one on the next page. Write your story question in the center balloon. Then make up answers to your question. Write the answers in the outer balloons.

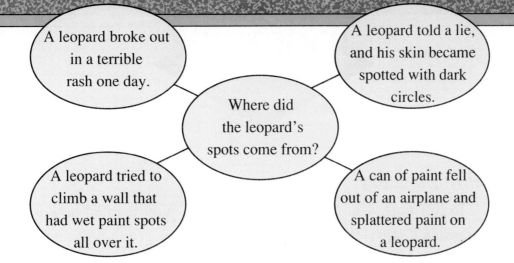

A leopard broke out in a terrible rash one day.

A leopard told a lie, and his skin became spotted with dark circles.

Where did the leopard's spots come from?

A leopard tried to climb a wall that had wet paint spots all over it.

A can of paint fell out of an airplane and splattered paint on a leopard.

Writing

Choose the answer you like best. Then build your story around it. You may begin with "Once upon a time . . ." or with your question. Then explain your answer. Be sure your story has a beginning, a middle, and an end.

Revising

Read your story. Is your question stated? Does it answer your question? Is your explanation clear?

Proofreading

Write a title for your tale. Then carefully reread your story. If you gave names to the animals, are the names capitalized? Copy your story neatly onto a sheet of paper.

Publishing

Enjoy a "Folk Tale Festival." Read your story aloud. Listen to your classmates' stories, too. Then display the tales on the bulletin board.

Telling a Story

In this unit, you met some storytellers. You learned how a professional storyteller tells stories. Now your group will retell one of the stories in the unit that you all liked.

Here are some things that your group should do as you work together:

♦ Agree or disagree in a nice way.

♦ Give suggestions to others.

♦ Listen when others are talking.

♦ Make sure everyone has a chance to practice.

Together discuss some of the stories you read in this unit. Choose one that all of you will retell. Will it be one with a lot of action? Will it be one with funny words? Think of ways to make the story interesting. Then each person in the group should tell a different part of the story. Remember that storytellers can ask listeners to join in by asking them to clap, wave, or answer questions!

Can you think of someone else who would like to hear your group tell its story?

BOOKS TO ENJOY

Thumbeline by Hans Christian Andersen *(Morrow, 1980)* This is a fairy tale about a very tiny girl who goes through many hardships and adventures until she is rescued by a swallow.

The Gift of the Sacred Dog by Paul Goble *(Bradbury, 1980)* This Native American legend tells how the Plains group got its horses. When the Plains people cannot find buffalo, a boy goes to the mountains to speak with the Great Spirit.

The Time-Ago Tales of Jahdu by Virginia Hamilton *(MacMillan, 1969)* Jahdu is upset at losing his shadow, and others make fun of him. He begins to think he has no special "gifts." But Jahdu *is* Jahdu and so regains his powers and also his missing shadow!

The Butterfly That Stamped by Rudyard Kipling *(Bedrick Books, 1982)* This tale is about a butterfly who "stamps." Find out how and why it got this habit.

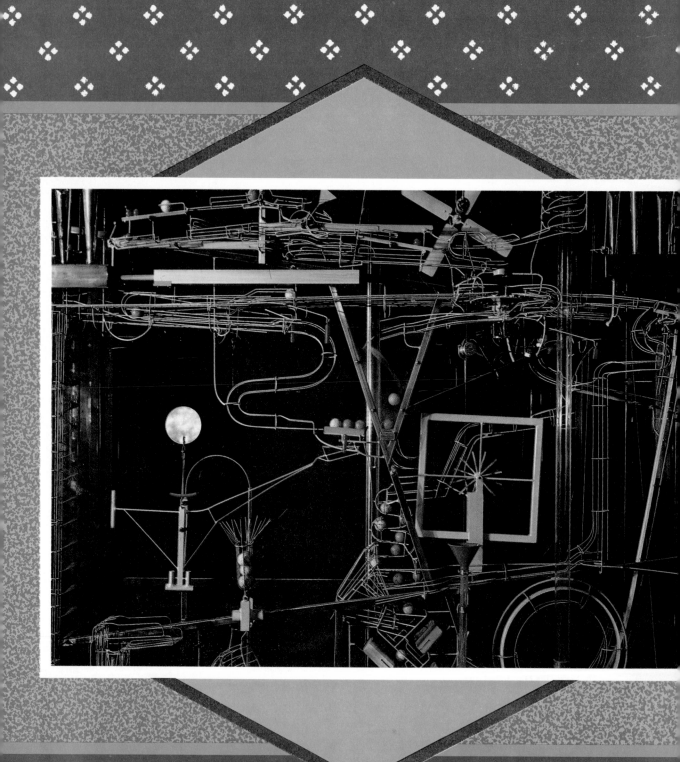

UNIT THREE

WORKING IT OUT

The world is full of puzzles and problems.

How do people work out their own solutions?

HAVING A BALL,
Multi-media sculpture by George Rhoads, American, 1984

A serious problem can bring out the best in people.
To solve her problem, Sybil must be stronger and braver
than she's ever been before.

Sybil Rides BY NIGHT

by Drollene P. Brown

It was the year 1777. The American colonists were
fighting to win their independence from Great Britain.
On the night of April 26, 1777, a man on horseback
came to the home of Colonel Ludington to tell him the
British were burning the nearby town of Danbury. The
rider was too tired to go on. Yet someone had to warn
the American soldiers. Sybil, the colonel's sixteen-year-
old daughter, said she would do it. Sybil and her horse
Star would have to ride all night.

170

Sybil swung up on Star. She patted his neck and leaned toward his ear. "This ride is for freedom," she whispered.

The colonel looked up at his daughter. He handed her a big stick. "Listen for others on the path," he warned. "Pull off and hide if you hear hoofbeats or footsteps or voices.

"You know where to go. Tell our soldiers that Danbury's burning. Tell them to gather at Ludingtons'." Sybil listened to her orders. She saluted her father, her colonel. He stepped back and returned the salute.

Sybil thought of what might happen. There were more than thirty miles to cover in the dark and rain. She could be lost or hurt or caught by redcoats! (The American colonists called the British soldiers redcoats because their jackets were a bright red color.) But she did not let these thoughts scare her. I will do it for the colonies, she said.

She turned Star south on a line with the river. There would be several lone farmhouses to alert before they reached Shaw's Pond.

It was almost eight o'clock when she reached the first farmhouse. Doors flew open at the sound of Star's hoofbeats.

Sybil shouted her message. She did not stop, but hurried on to the farmhouses that were along Horse Pound Road. It was about ten o'clock when Sybil reached Shaw's Pond.

The houses beside the water were dark for the night. Sybil hadn't thought of this. She had been so excited she had forgotten people would be sleeping.

Sybil stopped for only a moment. She led Star up to the door and pounded with her stick.

A window opened. A head poked out. "Look to the east!" Sybil shouted. "Danbury's burning! Gather at Ludingtons'!"

She did not beat on every door. She did not shout at every house. Neighbors called to each other; and in the little hamlets along her way, one of the first ones awakened rushed out to ring the town bell.

When the alarm began to sound, Sybil would stop her shouting and ride on into the darkness.

Her throat hurt from calling out her message. Her heart beat wildly, and her tired eyes burned. Her skirt seemed to be filled with heavy weights, for it was wet and caked with mud. She pulled her mother's cloak closer against the cold and rain that would not stop.

Sybil would not stop, either. All the soldiers in the regiment must be told. She urged Star on.

Outside the village at Mahopac Pond, Star slipped in the mud. He got up right away, but Sybil's eyes stung with tears. She would have to be more careful!

If Star were hurt, she would blame herself. She must walk Star over loose rocks and pick through the underbrush where there was no path.

Again and again, Sybil woke up sleeping soldiers. Nearing Red Mills, Star stumbled and almost fell. He was breathing heavily. "You are fine, Star," Sybil whispered.

More slowly now, they started on their way. Then—
hoofbeats on the path! Quickly Sybil reined Star to a
halt. She jumped down and pulled him toward the trees.

She held her breath and strained her eyes. Men
passed so close she could have touched them. They
looked like British soldiers, but sometimes skinners
dressed like soldiers of one army or the other to fool the
people they robbed.

Soon the hoofbeats died away. Sybil's hands and
knees trembled as she led Star back to the path.

"We'll make it," she softly promised him. Star
lifted up his ears and started off again. He was weary,
but he trusted Sybil.

When they reached Stormville, the alarm had already begun to sound. Someone from another village had come with the news. Sybil was glad, for she could only whisper. She had shouted away her voice.

Covered with mud, horse and rider turned home. When Sybil rode into her yard, more than four hundred men were ready to march. She looked at the eastern sky. It was red.

"Is Danbury still burning?" she asked and tumbled into Father's arms.

"No, my brave soldier. It is the sunrise. You have ridden all night."

"I do not feel like a brave soldier," Sybil whispered. "I feel like a very tired girl. Star needs care," she said sleepily as she was carried to her bed.

Early that morning, while that very tired girl slept, her father's men joined soldiers from Connecticut. They met the British at Ridgefield, about ten miles from Danbury.

The soldiers from New York and Connecticut battled with the redcoats. Most of the British escaped to their ships in Long Island Sound, but they did no more damage.

People spread the word of Sybil's ride. Soon General Washington came to her house to thank her for her courage. Statesman Alexander Hamilton wrote to her, praising her deed.

Sybil lived to be seventy-eight years old. Her children and her children's children loved to hear the story of a young girl's ride for independence.

◆ LIBRARY LINK ◆

If you want to know more about Sybil Ludington, you might like to read the whole book, Sybil Rides for Independence *by Drollene P. Brown.*

Reader's Response

What qualities of Sybil's do you admire?

Sybil Rides
BY NIGHT

Questions

1. Why did the American soldiers have to be warned?
2. Give three reasons why the ride was so difficult.
3. How did Sybil keep up her courage? What did she tell herself?
4. What might have happened if Star had been hurt?
5. What did the American soldiers do after they got Sybil's message? Explain how you got your answer.

Writing to Learn

THINK AND RECALL Map Sybil's ride for freedom. Draw an oval map and write the names of five places she visited. The first two have been filled in for you. Write a word to tell how Sybil felt at each place.

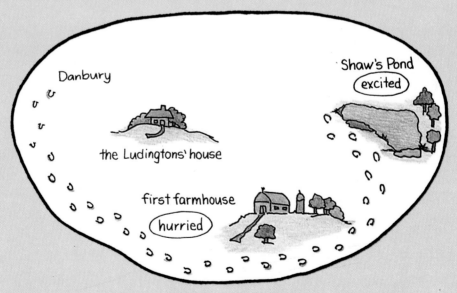

WRITE Use the words on your oval map. Write how you would feel if you were Sybil and went on her ride.

177

Does every problem have a solution? P'ei seems to think so. He tries to work out a problem that no one else can solve.

8,000 STONES

told by Diane Wolkstein
illustrated by Ed Young

Long ago in China, there lived a very powerful ruler. He was known as the Most Supreme Governor of China. His name was Ts'ao Ts'ao (tsäō tsäō).

Ts'ao Ts'ao ruled the royal city of Loyang (lō-yäng) and lived in a beautiful palace surrounded by lovely gardens. The treasures of the royal city and palace were protected by the Governor's mighty army of 10,000 soldiers.

But the neighboring kings and princes heard of Ts'ao Ts'ao's beautiful palace and mighty army, and they came themselves or sent messengers to see the wonders of the royal city.

The messengers often brought wonderful presents.

179

This year the Satrap, or prince, of India sent Ts'ao Ts'ao a most unusual present: a present that neither Ts'ao Ts'ao nor anyone in Ts'ao Ts'ao's kingdom had ever seen before. When the Indian messengers arrived in Loyang, the peasants came running from their fields to see the marvelous creature. The courtiers came out of the palace, and soon a huge noisy crowd formed around the animal.

Then Ts'ao Ts'ao appeared, and the Indian messengers, the peasants, and all the court knelt before him.

"Rise!" Ts'ao Ts'ao commanded the Indian messengers. "Rise and explain the cause of this uproar. What is this beast doing in my kingdom?"

"It is a present," explained the messengers. "It is a present from the Grand Satrap of India to the Most Supreme Governor of China, Ruler of Loyang, General of 10,000 soldiers—Yourself!"

"Oh . . . oh yes," muttered Ts'ao Ts'ao. (He just then remembered that this was the time of year the Satrap's presents usually did arrive.)

"Delighted!" exclaimed Ts'ao Ts'ao. "The Grand Satrap of India is to be informed that I am delighted with his . . . his . . . what is it called, his . . . ?"

"Elephant!" answered the messengers. Junma, the son of one of the Indian messengers, showed his small ivory elephant to P'ei (bāē), the son of Ts'ao Ts'ao. P'ei showed Junma his new Chinese sailboat.

"And how tall is my elephant?" asked Ts'ao Ts'ao.

"Ten feet tall, Most Supreme Governor of China."

"And how much does my elephant weigh?"

"Oh, we cannot tell you Most Supreme Governor. There are no scales in India large enough to weigh such an animal."

"You mean to say that the Grand Satrap of India does not know how much an elephant weighs?"

"That is correct, Most Supreme Governor of China."

"I see," said Ts'ao Ts'ao, "I see. . . ."

When the Indian messengers had been led into the palace to eat and rest, Ts'ao Ts'ao called his advisers together: "I want to know, before the messengers leave at the end of the month, the exact weight of my elephant. If the Grand Satrap of India does not know how to weigh an elephant, then I, Ts'ao Ts'ao, Ruler of Loyang, General of 10,000 soldiers, shall show him the way!"

The advisers then spent all their time thinking: How to weigh an elephant . . . ? How to weigh the Most Supreme Governor of China's elephant? How to weigh the elephant? But they could not think of a way. Then a week before the messengers were to leave, little P'ei came from playing with his sailboat to see the wonderful elephant.

"What are you doing under the elephant?" he called to the advisers.

"Shhh . . . we're thinking."

"What about?" whispered P'ei.

"How to weigh an elephant," the advisers whispered back.

"Well, that's not so hard," said P'ei.

"Not so hard?" cried the advisers.

"No," said P'ei. "Follow me, and I'll show you."

P'ei led them through the woods to a small pond near the palace. There by the pond was P'ei's new toy sailboat. It looked like any toy Chinese sailboat, except it had a strange line carved into its side.

"Wait here!" cried P'ei and he ran back to the palace.

The advisers picked up the boat. They looked at the line carefully. At the side of the line was the Chinese character for elephant.

What did it mean?

The advisers shook their heads.

They did not understand.

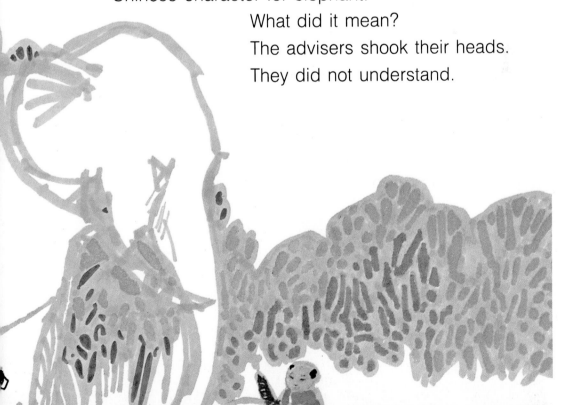

Little P'ei returned from the palace, carrying Junma's ivory elephant.

"Watch," he said to the advisers.

He placed the elephant on the sailboat and the boat sank in the water to the carved line.

"You see," P'ei explained, "no matter how many times I sailed Junma's elephant on my boat, it always weighed the boat down to that line, so I carved his character next to it. If you want to weigh the big elephant, you can do the same thing. And if you need to know the exact weight of the elephant, then pile stones on the boat until the boat sinks to the elephant's character."

"That's it! That's it!" cried the advisers. "Little P'ei, you've shown us the way."

On the day of the weighing, a large crowd of courtiers and peasants gathered around the shore of the palace lake.

The elephant was led from the fields onto a sturdy barge. Little P'ei and the advisers then stepped into a smaller boat.

Little P'ei was given the honor of carving, just above the water line, the character of the Most Supreme Governor of China's elephant on the barge.

After both boats were brought back to shore, the barge was pushed out again. Many stones were piled on it. It took many, many stones for the barge to sink to the character of the elephant. Can you guess how much the elephant weighed?

The elephant weighed 8,000 stones.

A gong was sounded and the announcement made by the court herald:

"The Most Supreme Governor of China's elephant weighs the Most High Amount of 8,000 stones!"

The peasants cheered and the courtiers applauded. The gong rang out again. This time Ts'ao Ts'ao, Most Supreme Governor of China, Ruler of Loyang, General of 10,000 soldiers, spoke:

"Let it be known that the plan for the weighing of the Most Supreme Governor of China's elephant was thought of by none other than my own son . . . little P'ei."

The peasants, the advisers, and the courtiers cheered even louder.

"AND let it be written in the court annals," continued Ts'ao Ts'ao, "and a copy be given to the Indian messengers to present to the Grand Satrap of India."

So the story of little P'ei and the weight of the elephant was written out and presented to the Indian messengers to take back to the Satrap.

And Ts'ao Ts'ao, Most Supreme Governor of China, then became famous—not only for his beautiful palace and mighty army—but also for the Most Supreme Intelligence of his clever son . . . little P'ei.

In later years, little P'ei became Ts'ao P'ei, EMPEROR OF ALL OF CHINA. That was in A.D. 200, almost 2000 years ago.

Reader's Response

Did it seem possible to you that P'ei could solve a problem that learned advisers could not?

8,000 STONES

Questions

1. Why did the gift from India cause such an uproar?
2. Why did Ts'ao Ts'ao want to find out the elephant's weight?
3. Why was the problem difficult to work out?
4. How did P'ei come to think of the solution?
5. Do you think that P'ei became a good emperor? How did you decide if he did or did not?

Writing to Learn

THINK AND RECALL   Writing can help you remember and understand what you read. Can you remember how P'ei solved the problem? How did P'ei decide to weigh the elephant?

WRITE   Write a sentence or sentences to tell how P'ei weighed the elephant.

READING FICTION

Vocabulary:

Synonyms and Antonyms

The city of Loyang in the story "8,000 Stones" was known far and wide for its many marvels. Read this sentence from the story.

> Ts'ao Ts'ao ruled the royal city of Loyang and lived in a beautiful palace surrounded by lovely gardens.

Suppose you wanted to replace the word *lovely* in the sentence with a word that means nearly the same thing. Which of these words would you choose?

> small   empty   pretty

You would use the word *pretty* because it is closest in meaning to the word *lovely*. Words that mean nearly the same thing are called synonyms.

How many synonyms can you think of for the word in italics in this sentence?

> The messengers often brought *wonderful* presents.

What would happen if you rewrote the sentence this way?

> The messengers often brought *terrible* presents.

Now the sentence has a different meaning. That is because *terrible* and *wonderful* are antonyms. An antonym is a word that means the opposite of another word.

Synonyms and antonyms may help you learn new words. Sometimes you can figure out what a new word means if you know its synonym or antonym. Look at this sentence from "8,000 Stones."

> This year the *Satrap,* or prince, of India sent
> Ts'ao Ts'ao a most unusual present . . .

Before you read the story, you may not have known who a Satrap was. The author included a synonym, *prince,* to help you understand the new word.

Using What You Have Learned

Read the paragraph below. First, write down a synonym for each word in italics. Then write down an antonym for each word in italics.

> "I'm so *glad* it's Monday," thought Maria. She
> got ready for school *quickly*. She was puzzled as she
> *shut* the front door. *No one* was out playing. The street
> was very *still.* Then she remembered. It was a holiday!

As You Read

Look for examples of antonyms and synonyms in the next selection, "The Ins and Outs of Measurement."

The Ins and Outs of Measurement

by Vicki Cobb

P'ei figured out a clever way to weigh an elephant in "8,000 Stones." We have different ways of measuring things today. Some of them are just as surprising as P'ei's way!

Sizing Things Up

Some things in the world are very, very big. The tallest mountain is Mount Everest, part of the Himalayan Mountains in Asia. It is as high as most jets fly. The Sears Tower in Chicago is now the tallest building. For forty years, the Empire State Building, in New York City, was the tallest. The largest ocean is the Pacific. The longest river is the Nile in Africa. The river with the most water is the Amazon in South America. Elephants and whales are the largest animals.

It is because things come in different sizes that we *measure* them. Measurement is used to answer questions like: How long? How short? How high? How wide? How heavy? How hot? How fast?

Measurement is important for some people when they work. A construction worker must know measurement to build houses and bridges. Butchers need measurement to know how much food they are selling. Scientists use measurement to learn about nature. Their measurements told us which was the tallest mountain and the largest animal.

People use measurement in their daily lives. When they shop, they tell storekeepers how much of something they want to buy. When they travel, they want to know how far they are going. When they know how hot or cold it is outside, they know how to dress for the day. When they cook, they have to know how to measure different amounts of food in order to follow a recipe. We can make appointments with a doctor, or a teacher, or a friend because we know how to measure time.

Different things are measured in different ways, so it is important to know many kinds of measurement.

Measuring by Weight

Another thing people measure is weight. Weight is the pull of the earth on objects near its surface. You can feel weight when you lift objects or when an object is resting on you. But people don't use the senses in their muscles to measure weight.

If you sit on one end of a seesaw and no one sits on the other end, your end will rest on the ground and the other end will be in the air. If you hang an object on a spring or a rubber band, the spring or rubber band stretches. The changes weight makes in the balance of a seesaw or the length of a rubber band or a spring led to the invention of tools for measuring weight.

Weight-measuring tools are called *balances* and *scales*. Balances and scales tell you how heavy or light something is by measuring distance.

You can make a simple balance out of a measuring stick. Tie a string around the middle of a yardstick, at the 18-inch mark. Leave enough string so that you can hold it, or tie the stick to some object. Make sure that the ends of the stick are free to swing up and down like a seesaw.

When the stick dangles freely, both ends should come to rest the same distance from the floor. In other words, the stick is balanced. If you hang an object on each end, the heavier object will be closer to the floor. When two objects have the same weight, the ends of the stick will be balanced.

Make handles on two paper cups, like the ones in the picture. You can now use your balance to weigh small things. Hang each cup one inch from each end. Your measuring stick should be balanced. Put a penny in one cup and a dime in the other. Which is heavier? Can you find some other small things to weigh?

There are many kinds of balances and scales. They all use units of measurement to tell just how heavy an object is. Long ago when people weighed things, they used handy objects like cereal grains or pennies to measure weight. You can see how by doing as they did with your measuring-stick balance.

Put a small object like a spool of thread or a pair of scissors in one cup of your measuring-stick balance. Which side of the stick is now closer to the ground? Now add, one by one, small objects that are alike, such as pennies or paper clips, to the other cup until the stick is balanced. A count of the number of pennies or paper clips needed to balance the stick is the weight of the object.

When people used handy objects for measuring weight, they had certain problems. Pennies, for example, come in different weights. An old, worn penny weighs less than a new one. So people finally decided to have standard units for weight.

A standard unit for weight is an object that is used only for weighing things. Weight units are usually made of metal that does not rust or change in any other way. A certain amount of sterling silver, for example, was called one *pound*. Although pound weights might be made of any kind of metal, every pound weight would balance a pound of sterling silver.

Another standard unit of weight is an *ounce*. There are 16 ounces in a pound, which means a 16-ounce weight balances a one-pound weight. Pounds and ounces are standard units in the English system.

Measurement is How to Know

Suppose someone said to you, "My dog weighs 30 pounds" or "That is a 20-inch bicycle wheel." You probably would not ask, "How do you know?" You know how people find out pounds and inches. If you think there may be something wrong about a measurement, you can get the right measuring tool and check for yourself.

Scientists use many measuring tools. A scientist who studies weather has a tool to measure the speed of the wind and another to measure the weight of the air. Scientists who study the stars have a tool that measures a kind of light, like x-rays, that is invisible to the human eye. Scientists who study what the earth is made of have tools that measure the size of atoms—tiny bits of matter that are difficult to see even with a microscope. Without these measuring tools, we would not know very much about wind speed, or the weight of air. We would not know that x-rays and atoms are real things.

Whenever scientists make a new discovery, someone almost always asks them, "How do you know?" A scientist cannot answer, "I just believe it." He or she must be able to answer, "I will tell you what I did to find out. If you do what I did, then you will know what I know."

You don't have to be a scientist to start inventing ways of measuring things. You can even use everyday measuring tools and standard units of measurement. You could measure how much rain fell during a storm by building a simple rain gauge. All you need is a can, such as a soup can, and a ruler. Stand the ruler straight up in the can.

Leave the can and ruler outside during a
storm. After the storm is over, measure how
deep the water is. If you do this for many
storms, you will find out that more water falls in
some storms than in others.

You can find out if beans give off heat as
they grow if you use a dairy thermometer.
Perhaps there is one in your school, or you can
get one in a hardware store. Soak some dried
lima beans overnight. The next day, drain the
beans and put them in a container that does not
let heat escape. A thick, lightweight, plastic cup
is good if you cover it with several thicknesses of
cardboard.

Make a hole in the cover so you can stick in the thermometer. Make sure the bulb of the thermometer is surrounded by beans.

Every morning read the thermometer and then check the beans to see how they are growing. After a day or so, if the beans seem dry, rinse them by putting them in a strainer and letting water run over them. Return the rinsed beans to the container. Keep a record of your temperature reading. You will find that the temperature goes up as the beans grow.

When you begin inventing your own ways to use measurement to learn about nature, you are thinking like a scientist.

 Reader's Response

What fact or facts did you read in the selection that surprised you?

The Ins and Outs of Measurement

Questions

1. What are four ways you use measurement every day? How did you think of your answers?
2. How did people weigh things long ago?
3. Why was it necessary to have standard units of measurement?
4. Invent a way to use everyday measuring tools to weigh a party balloon filled with helium.

Writing to Learn

THINK AND IMAGINE   Can you imagine what it would be like if we didn't have ways to measure certain things? Read the "what if's" below.

? ? ? ? ? ? ? ? ? ? ? ? ? ? ?

What if we did not have measurements for temperature?

What if we did not have measurements for weight?

What if we did not have measurements for distance?

? ? ? ? ? ? ? ? ? ? ? ? ? ? ?

WRITE   Answer one of the "what if" questions.
S-t-r-e-t-c-h your imagination to tell what might happen.

Comprehension:
Predicting Outcomes

In the story "The Ins and Outs of Measurement," you learned that scientists use tools to measure the speed of the wind and the weight of the air. This information helps them predict the weather.

When you read a story, you can also make predictions. Part of the fun of reading is guessing what will happen next. Then you can read on to see whether you were right, or whether the author surprises you. When you guess what will happen in a story, you are predicting outcomes.

Making Predictions

To predict outcomes, you have to be a detective and look for clues. You will find some clues in the story itself. Just ask, "What has already happened? What are the characters like? How do they behave?" Other clues come from what you know even before you start to read.

Think back to the story "The Emperor's Plum Tree." Remember when the emperor unrolled Musuko's scroll? He saw a beautiful drawing of a nightingale on a branch of the plum tree.

Did you predict what would happen next? The diagram on the next page shows some clues that you could have used to make a prediction.

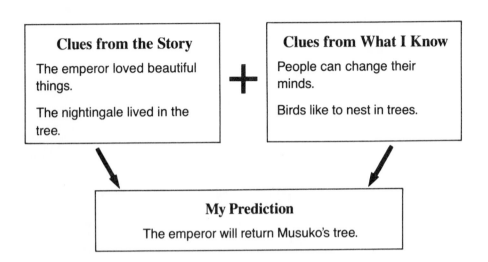

Clues from the Story		Clues from What I Know
The emperor loved beautiful things.	**+**	People can change their minds.
The nightingale lived in the tree.		Birds like to nest in trees.

My Prediction

The emperor will return Musuko's tree.

Using What You Have Learned

Read this story. Make a diagram like the one above to help you predict the outcome.

Kate's brother wanted to hear a bedtime story every night. Kate liked reading to her brother, but some nights she didn't have time because she had too much homework. When that happened, her brother was very sad.

One day Kate's teacher brought a tape recorder to class. The students had fun recording their own poems and plays. This gave Kate an idea.

As You Read

The next selection you will read is a play called "Fidelia." When you get to the end of each act, see if you can predict what Fidelia will do next.

*When Fidelia sets out to do something,
she just can't take ''no'' for an answer.*

Fidelia

by Ruth Adams
adapted by
Gary Apple

Characters:

Miss Toomey
Alberto (äl ber'tō)
Fidelia (fē dā'lē u)
Trombone players
Clarinet players
Carpenter
Papa Julio (pä'pä hōō'lē ō)
Carmela (cär mā'lu)
Drum players
Violin players
Shopkeeper
Mrs. Reed

Miss Toomey: (*to the audience*) Hello. My name is Miss Toomey. I conduct the school orchestra. Today, I'm going to tell you a story about the most interesting orchestra member I ever had. Her name is Fidelia Ortega (ōr tā′gu)! Fidelia came from a very musical family. Her father, Papa Julio, played the trumpet.

(Papa Julio *enters playing the trumpet.*)

Papa Julio: *Ta-ra-rar-ta! Ta-ra-rar-ta! Ta-ra-rar-ta!*

Miss Toomey: Fidelia's older brother, Alberto, was in my orchestra, too. He played the slide trombone.

(Alberto *enters playing his trombone.*)

Alberto: *Toom-room-room-room! Toom-room-room-room! Room-toom-room!*

Miss Toomey: Carmela, Fidelia's older sister, was also in my orchestra. She played the clarinet.

(Carmela *enters playing the clarinet.*)

Carmela: *Tootle-tee! Tootle-tee! Tootle-tum-tee!*

Miss Toomey: Yes, the Ortegas were a very musical family, except for little Fidelia. She didn't play a musical instrument.

(Fidelia *enters looking sad.*)

Fidelia: I want to make music too, Papa.

Papa Julio: You are too little, Fidelia. You will have to wait until you grow a little more.

Fidelia: But I don't want to wait!

Alberto: You can't play a trombone. (*He plays.*) *Toom-room-room!* Your arms are too short to work the slide.

Carmela: You can't play a clarinet. (*She plays.*) *Tootle-tee-tee!* You need all of your front teeth to play the clarinet.

Fidelia: I don't want to play a trombone or a clarinet. I want to play the violin!

Alberto: A violin? Don't be silly. Your arms are too short. Your hands are too small.

Carmela: You could not draw the bow or hold the strings down tight.

Papa Julio: They're right, Fidelia. Besides, you have to be in the fourth grade to play the violin in Miss Toomey's orchestra. I'm afraid you'll just have to wait.

ACT TWO

Miss Toomey: (*to the audience*) But Fidelia wanted to play the violin so badly, she could not wait. One day, she sneaked into the band room while my orchestra was practicing.

Drum Players: *Bump-be-dump! Bump-be-dump!*

Alberto and Other Trombone Players: *Toom-room-room-room. Toom-room-room!*

Violin Players: *Tink-plink-tunk! Tink-plink-tunk!*

Carmela and Other Clarinet Players: *Tootle-tee! Tootle-tu! Tootle-tee!*

Miss Toomey: Suddenly, our practicing came to a stop when we heard a loud CRASH!

(*A loud noise is heard.*)

Fidelia: Sorry. I tripped over the drums.

Carmela: Oh, no!

Alberto: Miss Toomey, this is my sister Fidelia.

Miss Toomey: Hello, Fidelia. What were you doing hiding behind the drums?

Fidelia: I want to play in your orchestra.

Miss Toomey: Do you, now? You're very young. What instrument do you want to play?

Fidelia: The violin!

Miss Toomey: Dear me, I'm afraid you are too small to play the violin, and it is very difficult to play. I'm sorry.

(Fidelia *sadly turns to leave.*)

Wait, Fidelia. I need a tom-tom player for the Indian dance we are learning. Would you like to play the tom-tom?

Fidelia: (*happy*) Oh, yes!

ACT THREE

Miss Toomey: (*to the audience*) And that's how Fidelia joined my orchestra. Fidelia enjoyed playing the tom-tom, but every week she would ask the same question.

Fidelia: (*to Miss Toomey*) Have I grown enough to play the violin yet?

Miss Toomey: (*to Fidelia*) No, not yet, Fidelia. (*to the audience*) Then, one day, I had some very important news to tell my orchestra. (*to the orchestra*) Boys and girls, Mrs. Reed, the director of the All City Orchestra, will be visiting us next week. She will choose the best musicians to be part of the All City Orchestra, so you must practice very hard.

Fidelia: I want to play for Mrs. Reed, too.

Alberto: But, Fidelia, you can't play a tune on the tom-tom.

Fidelia: Then I'll play a tune on something else!
(Fidelia *runs from the room.*)

ACT FOUR

Miss Toomey: Fidelia had a plan. On her way
      home, she stopped by a gift shop.
(Fidelia *enters the gift shop. A shopkeeper is
      unpacking a vase from a wooden box.*)
Shopkeeper: Can I help you, young lady?
Fidelia: Yes, I'd like to buy that box.
Shopkeeper: This box? You don't have to buy it.
      I will give it to you.
(*The* shopkeeper *gives her the box.*)
Fidelia: Oh, thank you!
Miss Toomey: (*to the audience*) Next, Fidelia
      stopped by a carpenter who was building a fence.

Fidelia: Excuse me. Might you have a small piece of wood that you can give me?

Carpenter: Sure, I have lots of wood pieces that I don't need. (*He hands her a piece of wood.*)

Fidelia: This will work fine. Thanks!

ACT FIVE

Miss Toomey: (*to the audience*) Fidelia ran home. She went into the garage, where she found a hammer and some nails. She tried to nail the board to the box, but had some trouble.

(Fidelia *hits her thumb with the hammer.*)

Fidelia: Ouch!

(Carmela *and* Alberto *enter.*)

Alberto: What are you doing in here?

Fidelia: I'm making something.

Carmela: What is it?

Fidelia: Do you promise not to laugh?

Alberto and Carmela: We promise.

Fidelia: I'm making a violin. But I can't get the nails to go in straight.

Alberto: Here, let us help.

Miss Toomey: (*to the audience*) Alberto and Carmela helped Fidelia build her homemade violin. It had nails for pegs, rubber bands for strings, and a clothespin for a bridge that the strings would go over.

Alberto: There, we're finished!

Carmela: Let's hear how it sounds.

Fidelia: OK, here I go. (*She plays her violin.*) *Twang-buzz-twank-thup.*

Carmela: (*She covers her ears.*) It sounds awful!

Fidelia: Maybe if I tighten the rubber bands it will sound better. (*She tightens them and plays again.*) *Zing-zong-zunk-zunk.*

Alberto: Well, it's better. But it still sounds pretty terrible.

Fidelia: I just have to practice a little more. (*She plays.*) *Zing-twang-zong-twang* . . .

Carmela: I can't stand it. I'm getting out of here. (*She leaves.*)

209

Alberto: Me, too. (*He leaves.*)

Fidelia: (*to herself*) It doesn't sound so bad to me. (*She begins to practice some more.*) Twang-boing-zang-zang.

ACT SIX

Miss Toomey: (*to the audience*) Fidelia practiced and practiced and practiced. Finally, the day for the All City Orchestra tryouts had come. (*to the orchestra members*) Children, I'd like you all to meet Mrs. Reed, the director of the All City Orchestra.

Mrs. Reed: Hello, students.

Orchestra Members: Hello, Mrs. Reed.

Miss Toomey: Mrs. Reed, to start with, the orchestra would like to play "The Man on the Flying Trapeze."

Mrs. Reed: Wonderful. I love that melody.

Miss Toomey: (*She waves her baton.*) Ready? Begin.

(*At the same time, the musicians play "The Man on the Flying Trapeze." All of a sudden, a strange sound comes from the back of the orchestra. It's* Fidelia *playing her homemade violin.*)

Fidelia: (*She plays.*) Buzz-zang-zong-zong-zing!

Miss Toomey: (*She taps her baton.*) Hold it! Stop! Stop! What ever is that noise?

Fidelia: It's me, Miss Toomey!

Alberto: Fidelia, oh no!

Carmela: Not here!

Miss Toomey: Fidelia, I should have known. Come over here, please.

(Fidelia, *with her homemade violin, goes to* Miss Toomey. Mrs. Reed *takes the violin from* Fidelia.)

Mrs. Reed: What is this, young lady?

Fidelia: It's a violin. I made it with some help from my brother and sister.

Mrs. Reed: It's very nice, Fidelia, but it doesn't belong in an orchestra. You can't play a tune on it.

211

Fidelia: Oh, but I *can* play a tune, Mrs. Reed. Listen! (*She begins to play "The Man on the Flying Trapeze."*) *Buzz-zang-zang-zoong-zing! Buzz-zang-zang-zoong-zing . . .*

(*Although the violin sounds strange, the melody of the song can be heard. When she finishes, everyone claps.*)

Mrs. Reed: That was very good, Fidelia! Where did you learn the correct hand positions for playing the violin?

Fidelia: I watched the other violin players. I did what Miss Toomey told them to do.

Mrs. Reed: How would you like to play a *real* violin, Fidelia?

Fidelia: I would love to, Mrs. Reed. But I'm too little, and not old enough yet.

Mrs. Reed: Oh, I don't know about that. (*to Alberto*) Are you Fidelia's brother?

Alberto: Yes.

Mrs. Reed: Well, I'd like you to do me a favor. My van is out in the parking lot. I'd like you to go there and . . . (*She whispers something in Alberto's ear.*)

Alberto: I'll be right back! (*He runs from the room, smiling.*)

Fidelia: Where is he going, Mrs. Reed?

Mrs. Reed: Just wait! You'll see.

Miss Toomey: (*to the audience*) None of us knew what Mrs. Reed was up to. Soon, however, Alberto returned, carrying the smallest violin case we had ever seen.

Alberto: Here it is.

Miss Toomey: (*to the audience*) Mrs. Reed opened the tiny case, and took out a beautiful little violin!

Mrs. Reed: This is a quarter-size violin, boys and girls. It is smaller than most violins. Let's see how it fits Fidelia.

Fidelia: (*She takes the violin and places it under her chin.*) It's perfect! My arms aren't too short, and it fits my fingers just fine!

Mrs. Reed: Fidelia, the boy who was using this violin has grown, so now he plays a bigger violin.

Fidelia: (*excited*) So you mean . . .

Mrs. Reed: That's right. How would you like to hold onto this one for awhile? Miss Toomey, do you think you can begin giving Fidelia violin lessons?

Miss Toomey: It would be my pleasure!

Fidelia: Does that mean I can play in the All City Orchestra?

Mrs. Reed: (*laughing*) No, not yet. But if you do as well as I think you will, I'm sure you will be in it next year.

Fidelia: Oh, boy!

Miss Toomey: (*to the audience*) But Alberto and Carmela *were* picked for the All City Orchestra that year. Fidelia and her father were proud of Alberto and Carmela as they performed in the concert. Fidelia didn't care if she wasn't in it this year. She had a violin exactly her own size, and her violin lessons had begun. As she clapped for her brother and sister, she knew that her day would come, too!

THE END

Reader's Response

Some people may think that Fidelia was a pest. What did you think of her? Why?

Fidelia

Questions

1. Why was Fidelia sad at the beginning of the play?
2. How did Miss Toomey try to help Fidelia?
3. How did Fidelia try to solve her problem?
4. When Mrs. Reed told Alberto to get something from her van, did you predict what it would be? How did you know?
5. Do you think that Fidelia went on to play in the orchestra? Explain why or why not.

Writing to Learn

THINK AND ANALYZE   Fidelia's dream of playing the violin is about to come true. Draw Fidelia. Write two sentences that tell what she did to achieve her goal.

She played the tom-tom. _____

She made a small violin. _____

WRITE   Have you ever wanted to do something very, very much? Write what you wanted to do. Tell how you tried to achieve your goal.

216

Imagine trying to make music without being able to hear. You may say it can't be done, but one man did just that.

Ludwig van Beethoven:

Master

of a Silent World

by Jeanette Leardi

In 1819, in the city of Vienna, Austria, Anton Schindler visited his friend Ludwig van Beethoven. When Anton arrived, Ludwig was playing the piano. The melody he played was beautiful, but there was something strange about the way he played the piano. As he played, he stamped his feet, and he sang out in a loud voice.

What was going on? Why did Ludwig stamp his feet and sing so loudly? Anton knew. His friend, the famous musician Ludwig van Beethoven (lōot'vik vän bā'tō vən), was writing a new piece of music. However, since Beethoven was completely deaf, he could not hear the loud sounds he made as he tried to imagine the sound of his music.

Beethoven's Early Life

How could this extraordinary man create music that he was unable to hear? Beethoven was not born deaf. He grew up hearing music practically all the time. He was born into a talented, musical family. His father, Johann van Beethoven, was a famous singer and a musician. He played the violin and clavier, an early form of piano. He was also a talented music instructor.

Beethoven learned to play music when he was a very young boy. He was only four years old when his father began giving him piano lessons. Soon after, he also learned to play the organ and violin. When he was only eight years old, he gave his first public concert, and by the time Beethoven was twelve, he was conducting an orchestra.

Beethoven loved to play music, but playing did not come easily to him. He had to practice for many hours. His hands were short, and sometimes he could not stretch his fingers to reach the notes that he wanted to play. Sometimes, when he found it difficult to play a piece of music, he would change the melody or make up a new melody. This surprised his teachers, but they knew that Beethoven had to be very talented to be able to do those things.

As Beethoven grew older, his father earned less and less money. Then, in 1787, his mother died. So Beethoven had to work hard to help support his father and his two younger brothers, Johann and Karl. To do this, Beethoven played in many, many piano concerts. Before long, his talent had made him famous.

Beethoven worked hard when he was composing new music.

Beethoven Creates Beautiful Music

In addition to playing music, Beethoven enjoyed creating new music. However, creating music was also difficult for him to do. It took him a long time to write a piece of music. Some of his greatest symphonies took him years to complete.

Why did it take Beethoven so long to write music? One reason was that he was very demanding of himself. He wanted each note to sound wonderful and important.

He usually started by writing bits and pieces of music. Then he would think about these short melodies and sometimes change them. Often he would cross out what he wrote and start all over again. A page of Beethoven's music looked messy and careless as he was writing it, but when it was finished and the music was performed, the sound that people heard was powerful and beautiful. They loved his music.

Beethoven Becomes Deaf

Music was the most important thing in Beethoven's life. Then, at the age of twenty-eight, he began to lose his hearing. At first, he heard a humming noise in his ears. Soon, he couldn't hear people when they talked softly to him. At the time, Beethoven thought that his problem was temporary and curable. But by 1801, the buzzing noise grew worse. It bothered him day and night. He tried everything he could think of to find a cure. He sought out doctors, and took special baths and medicines, but nothing worked.

Beethoven didn't want his friends to know that he was becoming deaf, so he stayed away from them. He no longer went to parties. He even took long walks in the countryside to escape the city noises that hurt his ears.

By 1802, Beethoven was so unhappy and angry that he almost decided to give up writing and performing music. In a letter to his brothers he wrote, "How terrible I feel that someone who stands beside me can hear a flute in the distance, or a shepherd singing, and I cannot." Beethoven did not know what to do.

Beethoven used an ear trumpet to improve his hearing.

Yet Beethoven knew in his heart that he was meant to write great music. So he decided that he would continue to write and perform. He also made up his mind to live differently. He began using a special object called an ear trumpet to hear what few sounds he could. He also carried a notebook or a chalkboard on which people wrote the things they wanted to say to him. He did eventually give up playing piano concerts, but he composed more music than he ever had before.

These are Beethoven's instruments.

Beethoven Composes His Greatest Music

In the years after 1802, Beethoven composed his greatest music. His love of music and his talent were so great that he didn't need his ears to hear the music he wrote. He listened instead with his mind and his heart.

By 1819, Beethoven was totally deaf, but his music was even more powerful than before. In 1824, Beethoven conducted an orchestra that was playing his Ninth Symphony for the first time. The symphony ended with a song of joy. When it was over, the audience stood up and clapped and cheered. However, Beethoven was not facing the audience, so he did not know how much they had enjoyed his music. Then one of the musicians on stage turned the great man around so he could see the audience. Beethoven saw the audience smiling and cheering wildly. Even though he could not hear his music, he could tell by the audience's reaction that it was very, very special. Without a doubt, Beethoven had learned to master his silent world.

 Reader's Response

What do you admire most about Beethoven? Why?

Ludwig van Beethoven: Master of a Silent World

 ## Questions

1. How did Beethoven show his musical talent when he was a child?
2. Why did it seem that Beethoven took a long time to write a piece of music? What makes you think so?
3. What did Beethoven do to hide the fact that he was becoming deaf?
4. How did Beethoven finally deal with the problem of being deaf?
5. Why is Beethoven's success so amazing?

 ## Writing to Learn

THINK AND RECALL The story of Beethoven is a great one. Copy the time line. Write important events from his life.

| 1787 | 1801 | 1802 | 1819 | 1824 |

Ludwig's mother died.

WRITE Make your own time line. Write one important event from each of the last three years of your life. Place these events and their dates on your time line.

Beethoven's Biggest Fan

Charles Schulz has entertained people with his *Peanuts* comic strip for a long time. We see Charlie Brown, Snoopy, Lucy, Schroeder, and the rest of the *Peanuts* gang in newspapers, books, on television, and at the movies.

Each of the *Peanuts* characters is special in some way. Snoopy would like to fly planes. Lucy likes to tell the others what to do. Charlie Brown wants everyone to like him. And Schroeder wishes he could play the piano like Ludwig van Beethoven. In fact, Schroeder is Beethoven's biggest fan. How can you tell? Read the comic strips on these pages for clues.

by Charles M. Schulz

From "Peanuts" by Charles Schulz. Reprinted by permission of United Feature Syndicate, Inc.

From "Peanuts" by Charles Schulz. Reprinted by permission of United Feature Syndicate, Inc.

Understanding Science Words

You read a science textbook somewhat differently from the way you read a story. When you read stories, you can usually get an idea of the meaning of words you don't know by using the clues in nearby sentences.

However, words used in science textbooks have exact meanings. It is important that you understand exactly what a science word means.

Learning the Meanings of Science Words

Science books give you the scientific meanings of words. Important words are usually printed in **boldface,** or dark type. A definition usually follows the boldfaced word. If a definition is not given, look up the word in a glossary or dictionary.

How can you find out and remember the meaning of a science word? Here are some steps you can follow.

1. When you see a boldfaced word, copy it onto a piece of paper.
2. Look for the word's meaning. Remember that the definition will usually be found in the same sentence or paragraph as the boldfaced word.

3. Write the meaning of the word on your paper.
4. Look for examples to help you understand the meaning of the word.
5. Pictures and drawings also help you understand the meanings. Look at the illustration and read the caption that tells about it.

Practicing the Steps

Now use these steps to understand how the word *force* is used in the following passage from a science textbook.

Picture someone pushing you on a swing or pulling you in a wagon. Sometimes you push to make things move, and sometimes you pull. You push or pull even when you lift something. A push or pull is a **force** (fôrs). Force is always needed to make something move.

In the passage above, the meaning of *force* is written in the same sentence as the boldfaced word. A force is "a push or a pull." The paragraph also gives you examples of force. "Someone pushing you on a swing or pulling you in a wagon" are examples of force that help you understand the scientific meaning. The picture of the dog pulling the boy is another example of force.

Read the following passage and look at the diagram.

Work is being done in the picture. Work is done when a force is used to move something. For example, you do work if you push a chair across a room.

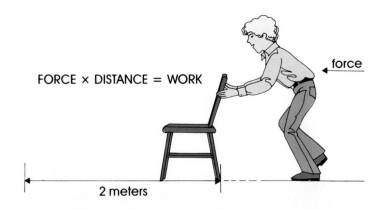

FORCE × DISTANCE = WORK

force

2 meters

The meaning of the word *work* is defined in the sentence after the boldfaced word. From the diagram you learn that *work* equals "force times distance."

You should also note that the word *force* is used in the definition for *work*. Learning the exact meaning of *force* earlier in this lesson helps you understand the exact meaning of the word *work*.

As You Read   Read the following pages from a science textbook. Then answer the questions on page 233.

The Lever—A Simple Machine

How does a lever help do work?

People do many kinds of work each day. Sometimes they use machines when they work. A **machine** is something that helps people do work. Not all machines are the same. Some machines, like cars, have many moving parts. Other machines have few or no moving parts. They are called **simple machines.** A snow shovel is a simple machine. How is it different from a snowplow?

Using a snow shovel

Using a snowplow

Using a lever

A **lever** (lev′ər) is a simple machine. Levers are often used to lift or move things. These children are using a lever to move a heavy rock. To do this work, they must use force to push down on the tree branch. The object that will be moved, the rock, is called the **load.** The force and the load move in opposite directions.

As the lever moves the rock, it moves on a turning point. The turning point here is the log. Levers always use a force, a load, and a turning point when work is done.

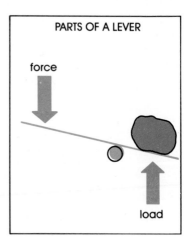

PARTS OF A LEVER

force

load

Using an Inclined Plane

How is an inclined plane used?

These people are using a ramp. A ramp makes it easier for them to put their things into the truck. A ramp is higher at one end than at the other. It is called an **inclined** (in klīnd') **plane.** An inclined plane is a simple machine. It can help in moving an object to a higher place.

Any slanted surface can be an inclined plane. A slanted board and a path going up a hill are both inclined planes. Some inclined

AN INCLINED PLANE

force

load

Using a ramp

Different kinds of ramps

planes are very steep. Others are not. It takes more force to move up a steep inclined plane. In all inclined planes the force and the load move in the same direction.

Inclined planes are used in many places. Some are ramps for cars and trucks to use. Others are ramps for people to use. Maybe some of your toys have ramps. Think of other places where you have seen inclined planes.

Two inclined planes together make a simple machine called a **wedge** (wej). They come together to form a V-shaped edge. A wedge can be used to cut and split things apart. An ax is a wedge. Would you be able to split wood with the other side of an ax?

Ax and log

Using What You Have Learned

1. What is a machine? How do you know?

2. What is a simple machine? What example is used to help you understand the meaning of a simple machine?

3. Look at the two illustrations used to help you understand what a lever is. How did the illustrations help you understand the meaning of the word *lever?*

4. What other boldfaced word appears on page 231? How did you find out what it means?

5. One kind of simple machine is the inclined plane. How did you find its scientific meaning?

6. How does boldfaced type help you in reading science?

7. What are three ways to find the meanings of important words?

Examples and excerpts are from *Silver Burdett & Ginn Science,* © 1987.

Helping someone in trouble is not always easy. It can even be dangerous. Doctor De Soto must decide if it is worth the risk.

Doctor De Soto

written and illustrated by William Steig

Doctor De Soto, the dentist, did very good work, so he had no end of patients. Those close to his own size—moles, chipmunks, et cetera— sat in the regular dentist's chair.

Larger animals sat on the floor, while Doctor De Soto stood on a ladder.

For extra-large animals, he had a special room. There Doctor De Soto was hoisted up to the patient's mouth by his assistant, who also happened to be his wife.

Doctor De Soto was especially popular with the big animals. He was able to work inside their mouths, wearing rubbers to keep his feet dry; and his fingers were so delicate, and his drill so dainty, they could hardly feel any pain.

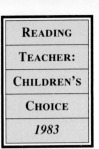
Being a mouse, he refused to treat animals dangerous to mice, and it said so on his sign. When the doorbell rang, he and his wife would look out the window. They wouldn't admit even the most timid-looking cat.

One day, when they looked out, they saw a well-dressed fox with a flannel bandage around his jaw.

"I cannot treat you, sir!" Doctor De Soto shouted. "Sir! Haven't you read my sign?"

"Please!" the fox wailed. "Have mercy, I'm suffering!" And he wept so bitterly it was pitiful to see.

"Just a moment," said Doctor De Soto. "That poor fox," he whispered to his wife. "What shall we do?"

"Let's risk it," said Mrs. De Soto. She pressed the buzzer and let the fox in.

235

He was up the stairs in a flash. "Bless your
little hearts," he cried, falling to his knees. "I
beg you, *do* something! My tooth is killing me."

"Sit on the floor, sir," said Doctor De Soto,
"and remove the bandage, please."

Doctor De Soto climbed up the ladder and
bravely entered the fox's mouth. "Ooo-wow!" he
gasped. The fox had a rotten bicuspid and
unusually bad breath.

"This tooth will have to come out," Doctor
De Soto announced. "But we can make you a
new one."

"Just stop the pain," whimpered the fox,
wiping some tears away.

Despite his misery, he realized he had a
tasty little morsel in his mouth, and his jaw
began to quiver. "Keep open!" yelled Doctor
De Soto. "Wide open!" yelled his wife.

"I'm giving you gas now," said Doctor
De Soto. "You won't feel a thing when I yank
that tooth."

Soon the fox was in dreamland.
"M-m-m, yummy," he mumbled.
"How I love them raw . . . with
just a pinch of salt."

They could guess what he was
dreaming about. Mrs. De Soto
handed her husband a pole to
keep the fox's mouth open.

Doctor De Soto fastened his extractor to the bad tooth. Then he and his wife began turning the winch. Finally, with a sucking sound, the tooth popped out and hung swaying in the air.

"I'm bleeding!" the fox yelped when he came to.

Doctor De Soto ran up the ladder and stuffed some gauze in the hole. "The worst is over," he said. "I'll have your new tooth ready tomorrow. Be here at eleven sharp."

The fox, still woozy, said goodbye and left. On his way home, he wondered if it would be shabby of him to eat the De Sotos when the job was done.

After office hours, Mrs. De Soto molded a tooth of pure gold and polished it. "Raw with salt, indeed," muttered Doctor De Soto. "How foolish to trust a fox!"

"He didn't know what he was saying," said Mrs. De Soto. "Why should he harm us? We're helping him."

"Because he's a fox!" said Doctor De Soto. "They're wicked, wicked creatures."

That night the De Sotos lay
awake worrying. "Should we let him
in tomorrow?" Mrs. De Soto wondered.

"Once I start a job," said the
dentist firmly, "I finish it. My father
was the same way."

"But we must do something to protect
ourselves," said his wife. They talked and talked
until they formed a plan. "I think it will work,"
said Doctor De Soto. A minute later he was
snoring.

The next morning, promptly at eleven, a very
cheerful fox turned up. He was feeling not a
particle of pain.

When Doctor De Soto got into his mouth, he
snapped it shut for a moment, then opened wide
and laughed. "Just a joke!" he chortled.

"Be serious," said the dentist sharply. "We
have work to do." His wife was lugging the
heavy tooth up the ladder.

"Oh, I love it!" exclaimed the fox. "It's just
beautiful."

Doctor De Soto set the gold tooth in its socket
and hooked it up to the teeth on both sides.

The fox caressed the new tooth with his
tongue. "My, it feels good," he thought. "I
really shouldn't eat them. On the other hand,
how can I resist?"

238

"We're not finished," said Doctor De Soto, holding up a large jug. "I have here a remarkable preparation developed only recently by my wife and me. With just one application, you can be rid of toothaches forever. How would you like to be the first one to receive this unique treatment?"

"I certainly would!" the fox declared. "I'd be honored." He hated any kind of personal pain.

"You will never have to see us again," said Doctor De Soto.

"*No one* will see you again," said the fox to himself. He had definitely made up his mind to eat them—with the help of his brand-new tooth.

Doctor De Soto stepped into the fox's mouth with a bucket of secret formula and proceeded to paint each tooth. He hummed as he worked. Mrs. De Soto stood by on the ladder, pointing out spots he had missed. The fox looked very happy.

When the dentist was done, he stepped out. "Now close your jaws tight," he said, "and keep them closed for a full minute." The fox did as he was told. Then he tried to open his mouth—but his teeth were stuck together!

"Ah, excuse me, I should have mentioned," said Doctor De Soto, "you won't be able to open your mouth for a day or two. The secret formula must first permeate the dentine. But don't worry. No pain ever again!"

The fox was stunned. He stared at Doctor De Soto, then at his wife. They smiled, and waited. All he could do was say, "Frank oo berry mush" through his clenched teeth, and get up and leave. He tried to do so with dignity.

Then he stumbled down the stairs in a daze.

Doctor De Soto and his assistant had outfoxed the fox. They kissed each other and took the rest of the day off.

◆ LIBRARY LINK ◆

William Steig has written and illustrated other books you might enjoy reading. One of them is Yellow and Pink.

 Reader's Response

What made this story funny to you?

Doctor De Soto

Questions

1. Doctor De Soto and the fox had mixed feelings about each other. What were these feelings?
2. What was the fox dreaming about? How did you figure out the answer?
3. Why was Doctor De Soto so sure the fox would eat him and Mrs. De Soto?
4. How did the De Sotos win out over the fox?
5. Why was the fox stunned at the end of the story?

Writing to Learn

THINK AND PREDICT   The fox was stunned when he discovered Doctor De Soto had tricked him. What might he say when he meets the mouse again? Draw two speech balloons.

WRITE   In the speech balloons you drew, write what you think the fox and the mouse will say the next time they meet.

Amy finds a wounded goose, and a challenge unlike any she has ever faced.

AMY'S GOOSE

written by Efner Tudor Holmes

illustrated by Tasha Tudor

Amy stood in the garden watching the sun sink behind the hills. She had been helping her parents dig the last of the potatoes. The air smelled of cool, damp earth mixed with the scent of the gold and orange leaves that fell silently and incessantly to the ground.

Then Amy heard the cry she had been waiting for all fall. Her face turned eagerly to the sky, and she saw the long V of the wild geese. Their call was faint at first, then louder as they flew closer. The cry fell down to her, carrying with it the spirit of all wild things. The geese began to break their formation as they came near the lake at the edge of the potato field. Amy knew that they would settle there for the night.

They always did and she had a large sack of corn in the barn, all ready for them. Usually a flock would settle at night and by daybreak be off again on its long journey south. Many times, in other years, Amy had seen the geese rise up through the morning mist. They would circle aimlessly for a moment and then the great long V would take shape and Amy would watch them as they flew away. In her mind, she could still hear their cry. To her, they seemed to be calling good-bye and she would be filled with loneliness. For Amy was an only child and the wild creatures were her friends.

But now the geese were over her, and coming in low. They were so close that Amy could feel the wind from their white wings. She stood, a small, still figure, as the geese flew past her and landed in the lake and on its shores.

Someone called to her and she turned to see her father walking down the garden. He stood beside her and put an arm around her shoulders.

"Well, little one," he said. "I see your friends have come back. As soon as we get these potatoes under cover and eat dinner, we'll get that sack of corn."

245

"Aren't they beautiful?" Amy asked him. "And there are a lot more of them this year."

Her father grinned down at her.

"That's because they've been spreading the word about a lake where a little girl will be waiting with a hundred pounds of good corn," he teased her. "Now come, it's almost dark and we've got to get these potatoes in."

Dinner seemed to Amy to be taking unusually long. Ordinarily she loved sitting there in the dining room with all three of them together, and the candles casting soft shadows on the warm wood-paneled walls. The room smelled of freshly baked apple and pumpkin pies. But Amy's thoughts were with the geese out on the moonlit lake. *Her* geese, she thought. They had remembered, and had come back to her again! She could hardly wait to go out to them, and to bring them some corn. It was a ritual she had kept up since one fall when the snow came early and some geese had stayed longer than usual. Amy had felt sorry for them and worried that they wouldn't have enough to eat. So she had scattered corn for them.

At last her father pushed back his chair and stood up. Amy got her sweater and followed him out to the barn. He hoisted the sack of corn to his shoulder and together Amy and her father walked down through the garden and into the field by the lake. The stillness of the night was broken only by the crickets singing their lonely song of the end of summer.

All at once they heard the frantic honking of a goose. Then the flock began to pick up its cry and Amy could hear their wings beating on the water. As she ran down the field she saw many geese rising up into the air in confusion and fright. Others stayed on the shore, standing with their long necks stretched low to the ground as they gabbled in alarm.

"It's a fox," her father cried. "Look, he's got
one." Dropping the sack of corn he picked up a rock
and flung it at the fox. Amy ran at him clapping her
hands and yelling. The fox let go of the goose and fled.
But the goose lay still. On its white neck Amy saw a
spreading spot of blood. She kneeled down and, as
gently as she could, she picked up the big bird. The
frightened goose beat its wings and tried to fly away but
it was too feeble to struggle for long. Soon it lay
quietly, its wings drooped over Amy's legs and onto the
sand. Amy's father squatted down to look.

"It may not really be as bad as it looks," he said.
"I think we can save her. Let's get her up to the barn."

He lifted the goose from Amy's arms and they
headed back up the field. Amy turned once to look
toward the lake. All was quiet again and Amy saw
several geese nibbling at the sack of corn they had
forgotten on the shore.

248

When Amy went to look at the wounded goose the
next morning, she was surprised to see it standing up
and pecking at a dish of feed. But it was obviously still
in some pain. Amy went slowly into the pen. She held
out her hand but the goose hissed at her fiercely and
retreated to a far corner. So the goose and the girl sat
for several minutes regarding each other.

"It's all right," Amy said softly. "You're safe here."

Amy spent most of the rest of the day with the goose. That evening the wild creature ate a few grains of corn from her hand. And when she stroked its head, the goose would gabble in what Amy felt sure was affection. A very special feeling for the big white bird was growing in her. She wondered hopefully if she'd be able to tame it. Amy thought it would be a real gift to have this wild bird place its trust in her.

For several days Amy was so busy taking care of her goose that she didn't stop to think it strange that the other geese had not left the lake to continue their journey to the warm South. One late afternoon, Amy and the white goose were out on the lawn. Amy was eating an apple and giving bits of it to the goose.

Suddenly they heard the cry of a goose overhead. Amy looked up to see a lone bird flying over the barn. It would circle silently, then start up its cry.

Amy's goose stood listening intently, with her head cocked to one side, looking up into the sky at the other bird. Then she began answering his call and flapping her wings. She ran over to Amy and nibbled at a piece of apple, but then she stood listening again. On the lake, Amy saw the rest of the flock. They had not left! They were waiting for her goose . . . and that must be her mate calling to her!

"Come on," she said to the goose, "I'm going to shut you up. You're not strong enough for flying yet. Next spring they'll be back."

Amy put the goose in its pen in the barn, closed the door firmly, and went to help her mother fix dinner. But all evening she felt upset. The warm house seemed to hold her in, like a cage. She thought of her goose, of the wild creature she had shut in the barn. She knew that the goose *was* really well enough for the long flight now. And she thought of the white gander flying alone over the barn calling to his mate.

She slipped out of the house and went through the shadow-filled garden and down to the lake. It was a cold night and mist was drifting up from the lake into the moonlight. Amy felt an eerie restlessness. Then she saw the geese. They, too, were restless. Several of them would rise up and call to the others, then drop back into the water. Others stood clustered on the shore as if holding a meeting.

Suddenly, they all rose up into the sky together. Their farewell cry filled the air and Amy watched them fall into flight formation. She would see no more geese until spring. Winter was coming. Amy knew it and obviously the geese sensed it, too. The flock had already grown small in the distant sky when Amy saw a lone bird drop out and begin flying back. Amy knew where it was headed.

She began running up the field. As she came to the barn, she heard the cry of the lone gander in the cold air and then the muffled honking that answered him from the barn. She flung open the door and ran to the pen where she had put her goose. The white goose was frantically pushing against the wire. When she saw Amy she stretched out her long neck and gabbled. Amy kneeled down. She put her arms around the big bird, and the goose put her beak in the curve of Amy's neck. Amy began to cry. She held the bird tightly, wishing it could stay. Then she picked up the white bird and carried her out into the night.

They stood silently together for a moment, until the goose set up a cry and began to run and beat her wings. Amy could hear the gander answering and as she watched, the goose rose into the moonlight. Her mate joined her and together they flew, following the flock before them.

Amy stood alone in the night and wiped away her tears. She felt the cold ground under her bare feet and thought of spring, when she would be standing by the lake watching a flock of white geese fly over her and into the water.

◆ LIBRARY LINK ◆

If you liked Amy's Goose, *you may want to read* Carrie's Gift, *a book written by Efner Tudor Holmes.*

Reader's Response

Do you think Amy made the right choice? Would you have done the same thing? Explain your reasons.

WRITING ABOUT READING

Writing an Explanation

In this unit characters solved their problems by learning to do new things. Remember P'ei? He figured out how to weigh an elephant by remembering what he learned when he played with the toy elephant. Dr. De Soto learned how to outsmart the fox and help him at the same time.

Think about a problem that you solved and what you learned as a result. Write a paragraph that tells about the problem and how you figured out the solution. Include a sentence at the end of the paragraph that tells what you learned.

Prewriting

Think of a problem you have faced. Here are some ideas.

- helping a sick animal

- finding something that is lost

- fixing something that was broken

Draw a picture of yourself solving the problem. Next to the picture, write a sentence that summarizes how you solved the problem.

Jeff solved the problem of getting places by learning to ride a bicycle.

Writing

Write a paragraph that explains the problem you faced. Be sure to tell how you solved it, and what you learned.

Revising

Read your paragraph aloud. As you read, listen to your words. Have you left out a word or a phrase? If so, add it now.

Proofreading

Have you indented your paragraph? Have you used a dictionary to correct spelling? Does each sentence start with a capital letter and end with a period? Copy your paragraph neatly on a sheet of paper.

Publishing

With your classmates, make a ''Problem Solvers'' bulletin board. Put your paragraph on the bulletin board. Add the picture or drawing you made that shows you solving the problem.

WORKING TOGETHER

Working out a Solution

In this unit, you read about people working out their problems. Now see if your group can work together to write a plan for solving a problem.

Here are some things that your group can do to work well together:

- ◆ Help everyone give ideas.
- ◆ Respond to other people's ideas.
- ◆ Pay attention when others are talking.
- ◆ Make sure the group finishes on time.

As a group, think of some problems to work on, such as how to get to know a new classmate better.

How We could get to know a new classmate:
1. Eat lunch together
2.
3.

Together, decide on one problem to work on. Then think about what you could do to solve it. Take turns making suggestions. The more ideas you can think of, the better, because there is usually more than one way to solve a problem.

Choose one of the ideas. Then work together to write a plan for solving the problem. Finally, share your solution with one other group.

Birdsong by Gail E. Haley *(Crown, 1984)* When a young girl plays the pipes, all kinds of birds come to her. Jorinella, a bird-seller, befriends the girl so that he may capture the birds. Will the girl find out the truth about Jorinella?

Perfect Crane by Anne Laurin *(Harper & Row, 1981)* A magician is lonely, so he brings a paper crane to life. They become friends, but the magician knows that the crane must be free to be happy.

Annie and the Old One by Miska Miles *(Little, Brown, 1971)* Annie's grandmother is dying, and Annie cannot stop the cycle of life and death.

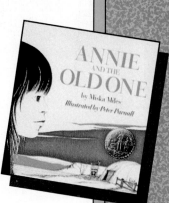

The Tale of Meshka the Kvetch by Carol Chapman *(E.P. Dutton, 1980)* Meshka is always complaining. One day her tongue starts to itch and her complaints begin coming true. When she talks about the good things in her life, her complaints disappear and her tongue stops itching.

WEATHER OR NOT

Come rain, come snow, come heat, come hail...

Why is everybody interested in the weather?

UMBRELLAS IN THE RAIN,
painting by Maurice Prendergast,
American, 1899

People have been talking about the weather for a long time. Maybe Aesop started all the talk in this fable.

The Wind and the Sun

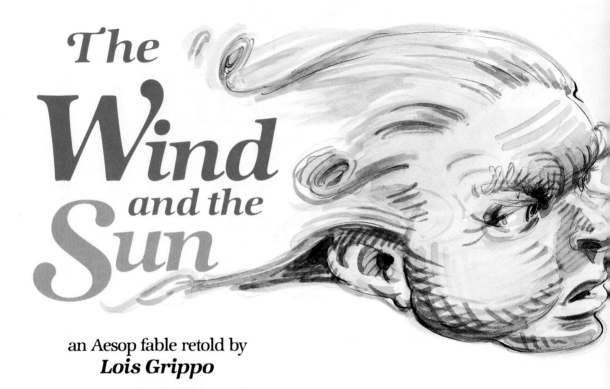

an Aesop fable retold by
Lois Grippo

Sun was smiling to herself in the morning sky. She had just woken up and was about to share her bright smile with the earth. Suddenly, there was a great whoosh of air. The whoosh was so strong that it blew a cloud right across Sun's morning face.

"Good morning, Sunshine," a voice boomed out. It was Wind. "How are you today, my little friend?" she whooshed. "As a matter of fact, where are you?" Wind said. "You seem to be covered by a cloud." Then Wind threw back her curly head and laughed. She laughed so hard, the cloud in front of Sun's face blew right away.

Sun smiled kindly into Wind's face. "Good morning, Wind," she said. "Are you all right? You seem all out of breath! Did you use too much of your strength blowing that cloud in front of my face?"

"If you think that took strength, you are not as bright as you think," Wind puffed. "All I did was yawn."

Sun smiled so sweetly that all the flowers on the earth popped out of the ground and looked up at her. "Oh, my," she said. "Sometimes I forget my own strength. It is much too early for the flowers to bloom."

"You call that strength!" Wind shouted. Then she breathed in very deeply and let out a powerful gust of air. The poor flowers shook. Their petals blew off and whirled in the air. Even the trees shook and bent. "Now that's strength," Wind boasted. "And I hardly even tried."

"Oh, Wind," Sun said. "Don't be so puffed-up all the time. You are strong, that's true. But, I am stronger."

"Come on, Sun," Wind said. "Don't get so hot under the collar. You are strong, I suppose. But, *I* am stronger!"

Now, Wind and Sun had argued many times about who was stronger. Wind would huff, and Sun would sweetly shine. Wind would puff, and Sun would sweetly shine. It seemed like an argument that had no winner. Then one day, Sun had an idea.

"Let's have a contest," Sun said to her windy friend.

"It will be no contest at all," Wind boasted. "I will win, of course. You will learn once and for all that I am the stronger!"

Sun just smiled calmly. She filled the sky with her warm rays.

"What will the contest be?" Wind asked.

Sun looked down and saw a man with a long beard walking down the road. He was wearing a heavy cape around his shoulders. "See that man," Sun said to Wind. "The contest will be to see who can make him take off his cape."

"Good!" said Wind. "That should take me just a second or two. I am in a hurry, you know. I have to start a hurricane this afternoon."

"Since you are in such a rush," Sun said, "why don't you go first?"

"That's fine with me," Wind said. "Watch this!"

Wind caught some air in her cheeks and began to puff up. She blew up like a balloon. Then, Wind opened her mouth and out rushed a gust of air. When the air reached the earth, the man's hair began to blow a bit, but he didn't even notice.

"I was just warming up a bit," Wind said. "Now, I'll really get to work."

With that, Wind blew even harder. Everything shook. Windows rattled. Tree branches snapped. The air was full of flying objects. The man's hair and beard blew this way and that. His hands grew cold, and his face burned from the wind. But the man did not lose his cape. He held it tightly around him. The harder Wind blew, the colder the man became and the tighter he clung to his cape.

"Would you like to rest awhile and catch your breath?" Sun asked.

"Don't get so overheated," Wind growled. "I was just trying to make the contest exciting. Now, I'll show you what I can really do."

Wind took a deep, deep breath. She drew in great mouthfuls of air until she was bigger than the world's largest blimp! Then, she opened her mouth. There was a tremendous roar as all the air rushed out.

Dark storm clouds filled the sky. The whirling, swirling air hit the earth. It blew so hard that the water in the lakes turned into great waves. Huge oak trees were bent in half. Birds that were flying south were pushed backward toward the north. Still the shivering man did not lose his cape! The fierce winds just made him hold on to it even more tightly.

At last, Wind was tired out. She was too tired to blow even the tiniest breeze. Everything on the earth stood still. The storm clouds slowly drifted away. It was Sun's turn.

Sun calmly turned her face toward the earth. She gently shone down on its green fields. She gently shone on the man walking down the road. The man raised one hand to cover his eyes. With the other hand, he still held on to his cape.

"See! See!" said Wind. "You are no stronger than I am." Wind was still very tired. Those few words took all the breath she could manage.

Sun smiled calmly at her worn-out friend. "Just rest," she said. "I will try again."

Sun turned back to the earth. She shone more brightly. The air grew warmer and warmer. Soon the man began to feel more comfortable. He undid the buttons on his cape, though he still held on to it with one hand. Sun was not upset, but Wind was starting to get back some of her strength.

"Face it!" Wind breezed. "If I could not loosen his cape, surely you cannot."

Sun did not lose her temper. She just continued to smile warmly down on the man. The warmth of her rays caused the man to become very hot. The man smiled in Sun's pleasant warmth. Soon he was too hot to keep his cape on. The man gladly removed it from his shoulders.

"See!" said Sun. "Now tell me which of us is the stronger!"

Wind looked as though all of the air had gone out of her. For once, she had absolutely nothing to say. Wind knew all too well who had won the contest. Sun was the stronger!

LESSON: You can do more with gentleness than you can do with force.

◆ LIBRARY LINK ◆

Aesop lived in Greece more than 2500 years ago. If you would like to read other fables by Aesop, try The Fox and the Crow, The Lion and the Mouse, *and* The Boy Who Cried Wolf.

Reader's Response

What do you think of the lesson this story teaches?

The Wind and the Sun

Questions

1. Why did Sun and Wind have a contest?
2. What did each one try to do?
3. Which did you expect to win? What made you think so?
4. What did Wind think would happen when she blew harder and harder?
5. What really did happen?
6. What one word would you use to describe Sun? What one word would you use to describe Wind?

Writing to Learn

THINK AND COMPARE   In this fable, the Wind and Sun appear as people. How are they alike? How are they different? Copy and add to the chart below.

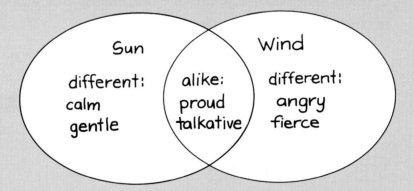

WRITE   Use the information on your chart. Write an introduction. Present either Sun or Wind to your classmates. Begin with "Meet Wind . . ." or "Meet Sun. . . ." Then tell more about the one you chose.

267

Study Skill:

Bar Graphs

One minute it was cold enough to freeze water! The next minute it was hot enough to fry an egg! That's what the temperature must have felt like to the man in "The Wind and the Sun." What is a good way to show these changes in temperature? A bar graph is, because it shows information in a way that is easy to read and compare.

Look at the bar graph below. The title and the labels tell what kind of information is shown. This bar graph shows the temperatures on the day Sun and Wind had their contest. The numbers on the bottom of the graph give temperatures in degrees Celsius.

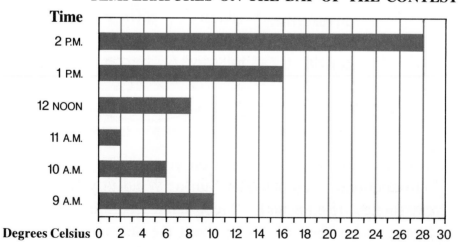

TEMPERATURES ON THE DAY OF THE CONTEST

268

Each bar on the graph stands for a different temperature. To read the graph, follow each bar to its end. Then run your finger straight down to the number at the bottom of the graph. The number tells the temperature shown by the bar.

> **STEPS FOR READING A BAR GRAPH**
> 1. Read the title and labels on the graph to learn what kind of information is shown.
> 2. Follow a bar to its end. Then trace your finger to the number line to read the amount that the bar stands for.

Using What You Have Learned

Study the bar graph below. Then answer the questions.

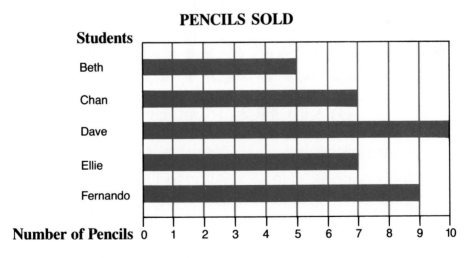

PENCILS SOLD

1. What kind of information does this graph give you?
2. Who sold the most pencils?
3. Which two students sold the same number of pencils?

Everyone wants to know about the weather, but no one wants to know more about it than Mr. Dreumont. He's a meteorologist, and it's his job to find out what the weather will be.

AN INTERVIEW WITH A

Meteorologist

BY GEORGE PORTER

George is fascinated by the way weather changes. He wants to know about weather and how meteorologists, people who study the air that surrounds the earth, forecast changes in the weather. A friend of his parents, Antonio Alfonso Dreumont, is a meteorologist. For a science project at school, George wrote to Mr. Dreumont to ask if he could interview him. Mr. Dreumont agreed.

GEORGE: Where did you grow up?

MR. DREUMONT: I grew up in Brownsville, a city on the southern coast of Texas.

GEORGE: Did the weather there make you curious about how and why weather changes?

MR. DREUMONT: Yes! The weather in South Texas often changes very quickly. A day can start out warm with clear skies, and by the afternoon there is thunder, lightning, and pouring rain. These sudden changes fascinated me, and made me very curious about the reasons for changes in the weather.

GEORGE: How long have you been a meteorologist?

MR. DREUMONT: I have been a meteorologist for 24 years.

GEORGE: When did you first decide to become a meteorologist?

MR. DREUMONT: The idea first came to me when I was in high school. I had to write a term paper on hurricanes. It was the first time that I did research on weather. I used books and magazines, reading everything I could find about hurricanes. The more I read, the more I wanted to read. I knew then that when I went to college, I would study meteorology. After college, I became an assistant at the Brownsville Weather Bureau.

GEORGE: What did you learn at the Brownsville Weather Bureau?

MR. DREUMONT: It was there that I really learned how to be a meteorologist. I learned how to tell airplane pilots about weather conditions. It was my job to give pilots a description of the kinds of weather they were flying into. I also learned how to make farming forecasts. These forecasts warned farmers if the land was too cold to start planting, or when it was wet and warm and therefore a good time to plant. Perhaps the most important thing I learned was how to read radar. Radar makes it possible to see conditions that affect the weather, beyond what you can see with your eyes.

wind speed 80 mph

Tornadoes can cause a lot of damage.

GEORGE: Where else have you worked?

MR. DREUMONT: I have worked in many different places. I worked in Georgia, where I saw thunderstorms and tornadoes. I worked in San Francisco, California, where the weather is ideal. It never gets too hot or too cold, and most of the time the sun is shining. I worked in Washington, D.C., at the National Headquarters of the Weather Service. Then, in 1981, I moved to Boise, Idaho. There I began to specialize in forecasting forest fires.

GEORGE: How do you forecast forest fires?

MR. DREUMONT: Idaho is in the northwestern part of our country. The weather here is sometimes very dry. If we have a mild winter, there is little snow to melt in the spring. Therefore, the trees and grasses tend to be very dry. This becomes a problem when we get dry thunderstorms. During a dry thunderstorm, rain evaporates before it hits the ground and strong winds push lightning bolts toward the ground. When that happens, the chance of forest fires increases. When I see those conditions, I warn people about the danger of possible forest fires.

GEORGE: Have you shared your experience forecasting forest fires with other meteorologists?

MR. DREUMONT: Yes! Because I speak Spanish, I have had the opportunity to teach courses on the detection and prevention of forest fires in Ecuador, Chile, Argentina, Venezuela, and Spain. Working in all of those countries has made it possible for me to meet and talk with many other meteorologists. Together, we talk about the problems we share in forecasting weather, and the use of new technology to help solve those problems. These experiences have helped me to become a better meteorologist.

GEORGE: What do you do on a typical day at the National Weather Service in Boise?

MR. DREUMONT: The first thing I do is use the computer to check weather forecasts and to look at weather maps of the atmosphere. The atmosphere, or the air that surrounds the earth, is described in numerical units on the computer. These units tell about the conditions in the atmosphere. I use that information to lead a staff discussion on weather conditions. We talk about whether the rivers are high and could cause flooding. We decide if wind conditions may cause problems for airplane pilots. If it's the fire season, we talk about the kind of weather conditions that increase the chance of fires. Then we send up a weather balloon that carries an instrument called a radiosonde. The radiosonde measures temperatures, wind, humidity, or moisture in the air, and atmospheric pressure in the upper atmosphere. Then we use the information gathered by the radiosonde to forecast the weather.

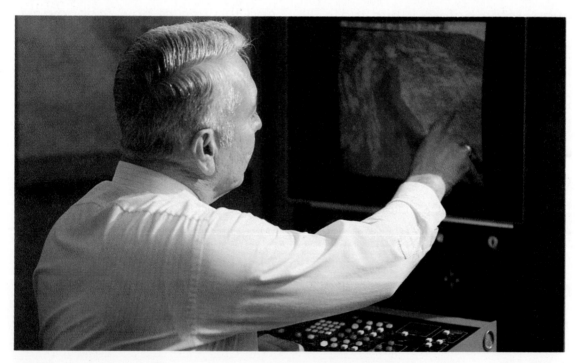

Mr. Dreumont checks a map on his computer screen.

Mr. Dreumont releases a weather balloon.

GEORGE: What other instruments do you use and what information do you get from them?

MR. DREUMONT: We use a ceilometer to tell us the height of the clouds from the ground. This information is important for pilots. If the clouds are too close to the ground, pilots might have trouble seeing the runway as they prepare to land. To check the temperature, we use wet and dry bulb thermometers. The anemometer measures wind speed, and the weather vane shows the wind's direction. Humidity is measured by a hygrometer. And we use computers to find out the relative humidity, or the amount of moisture in the air in relation to the temperature.

GEORGE: Do you use computers to forecast the weather?

MR. DREUMONT: Yes, we do. Computers are one of the most important tools meteorologists have. Computers can give us a reasonable guess as to what tomorrow's weather will be. But it is up to the meteorologist to check the accuracy of the computer. He or she does that by looking at the numerical units that the computer uses to describe the atmosphere, and then evaluating those units based on additional information that is supplied by weather instruments. Together, this information makes it possible for a meteorologist to forecast the weather.

GEORGE: How does weather forecasting help people?

MR. DREUMONT: People in many industries make

decisions based on weather conditions. Farmers need to know when a cold front is coming so they can protect their crops. Airlines need to know if stormy weather will delay flights. Construction workers cannot build homes if the weather is too cold or too wet. You and I need to know if there is an emergency, such as a hurricane or a flood.

GEORGE: What are the hardest things to forecast?

MR. DREUMONT: Big events, such as floods, droughts, and blizzards, are difficult to forecast. Deciding when rain will turn to snow is difficult. It can also be hard to forecast when the temperature will drop to its lowest point during the night.

◄ **Instruments help meteorologists forecast the weather.**

Mr. Dreumont takes time to enjoy some sunny weather.

GEORGE: Why do you like being a meteorologist?

MR. DREUMONT: My job is fun all the time. No two days are ever alike. Weather is not only my job, it is my hobby. For 48 years of my life, meteorology has been my love. I love to go out in the middle of the night to watch a thunderstorm. I love to look out my window and watch the beauty of a snowstorm. The beauty of nature and the changes that weather brings make my job interesting to me.

 Reader's Response

What do you think is the most fascinating part of Mr. Dreumont's job? Why?

AN INTERVIEW WITH A
Meteorologist

Questions

1. When did Mr. Dreumont decide to become a meteorologist?
2. How did working in many different places make Mr. Dreumont a better meteorologist?
3. Who are some of the people who depend on weather forecasts to do their job?
4. Why do you think meteorologists can forecast the weather more accurately today than years ago? What led you to your answer?
5. What kind of weather facts might a meteorologist show on a bar graph?

Writing to Learn

THINK AND QUESTION By asking questions, George learned a lot about the meteorologist. Look at the list below. It contains some of the questions he asked.

George's Questions for the Meteorologist
- Where did you grow up?
- When did you first decide to become a meteorologist?
- What do you do on a typical day at the Weather Service?

WRITE Think of someone *you* would like to interview. It might be a teacher, an athlete, or the president! Write the name of the person you would like to interview. Then write three questions you would ask in the interview.

Buried Treasure in the Library

W here do you think treasure hunters begin to search for sunken treasure? On the bottom of the ocean? Stop and think again. First they have to know where they are likely to find a sunken ship and whether it might be filled with gold and silver. The main place to find that out is in books.

That is why treasure hunters spend as much time in libraries and museums as they do under the water. Consider the story of Kip Wagner, who lives in Sebastian, on the east coast of Florida. One day when he was diving in the ocean he found some gold coins dated 1714. He thought they might have come from sunken Spanish ships, but he was puzzled. He had read that the galleons, which had sunk in 1715, had gone down either north or south of Sebastian. Could those books have been wrong?

▲ Bad weather caused some treasure-filled galleons to sink in the Caribbean Sea.

Floriano Caballero, Director, works in a special library in ▶ Burgos, Spain.

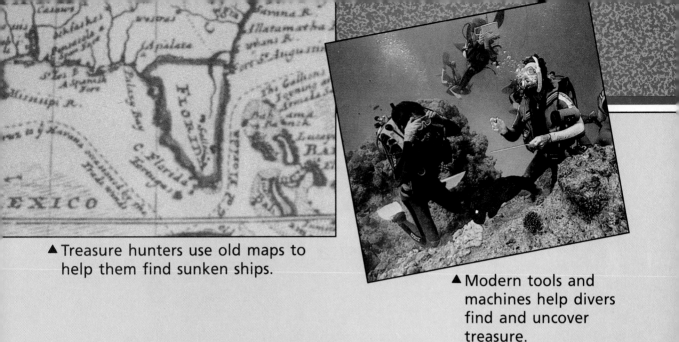

▲ Treasure hunters use old maps to help them find sunken ships.

▲ Modern tools and machines help divers find and uncover treasure.

The only thing to do was to look for some more information. Kip's friend, Dr. Kelso, went to the Library of Congress in Washington, D.C. He found a very old book about Florida with a map of the east coast made in 1775. The map showed that the boats had really sunk right off the coast of Sebastian.

Just to be sure that they were on the right track, Dr. Kelso went to Spain, where the ships had set sail. He spent many long hours checking old maps and other records in libraries there. Finally, when Kip Wagner and Dr. Kelso were sure, they bought a boat, hired divers, and began their underwater search.

At the end of six years, Kip Wagner's crew had found sixty thousand gold and silver coins, jewelry, and many bars of gold and silver. Then, after all that work, books helped Kip Wagner again. By reading books about jewelry and coins and other treasures, he knew what they had found and how valuable it was. Kip Wagner would tell you that the place to start looking for treasure is in books.

▲ Mel Fisher's library research helped him find gold and silver worth more than a million dollars.

281

Mississippi Possum

by Miska Miles

When heavy rainstorms cause rivers to rise, people are in danger, and so are animals. Imagine how a little possum feels as the rising Mississippi creeps toward his home.

Near the Mississippi River, a little gray possum lived in a hollow log.

When he was afraid, which was much of the time, he crept into the log and waited there.

He was afraid of many things. He was afraid of hawks and owls, of bobcats and foxes. And he was afraid of people.

When people came near, he ran into the log and was as still as he knew how to be.

There were things he was not afraid of. He was not afraid of mice or snakes, birds' eggs or berries. These, he ate.

Now, for a long time the rain had fallen and the river water rose and spread out farther along the banks. The possum looked around for food, for he had found nothing to eat for a day.

He looked up into a tree that grew beside the river, and he knew there was a bird's nest high in the branches.

He climbed up above the nest, and held a branch with his back foot, and swung by his tail to look into the nest. The nest was empty.

He climbed down again, and he looked around for berries. While he was looking he felt the earth tremble with footsteps, and he knew that something was coming down the hill, and he was afraid. He ran into his hollow log and was as still as a wild animal can be.

Jefferson Jackson and his sister Rose Mary came down the hill to look at the river.

"Look at that old Mississippi," Jefferson said. "It's getting higher and higher."

For a minute they watched. "It's coming this way," Rose Mary said. She pointed to a little stick lying on the ground. "Watch. The water's touching it." They waited.

"And now the stick's floating off," Jefferson said. "River's coming. Let's tell Papa."

They ran, pounding their feet hard against the ground.

When everything was quiet, the possum came out from his log. The brown river water was creeping along the ground toward him. Now a leaf held it back, then on it came, pushing its slow way—

He turned to go up the hill.

He traveled a long time and he came to a little brown house. He hurried past, for he knew that people lived there.

In this house, Jefferson and Rose Mary were talking to their mother and father.

"We could see the river coming higher while we watched," Jefferson said.

"Right up the hill," said Rose Mary.

"We know," said their mother. "We were about to look for you. We're going up to higher ground, where it's safe."

"The news came over the radio," their father said. "Everybody has to get out. The river's so high that it's breaking through the levee. If it breaks in many more places, it could flood right over this land. Hurry."

"Will we come back?" Rose Mary asked.

"We'll be back when the river goes down," her father said.

"That old river will pour a lot of water into the Gulf of Mexico," Jefferson said. "Then everything will be just as it's always been."

Now, all this time the possum was trudging up the hill, and he saw many things.

He saw a rabbit and a dog traveling along together and the dog didn't chase the rabbit. He saw a fox and a wild turkey and the fox didn't kill the turkey.

And behind him he heard the river, and he knew he must run from it.

He heard something coming close behind him. Something else was running from the river.

There was no tree he could climb and the grasses were not thick enough for hiding. He lay down on the ground and he didn't move.

Rose Mary and Jefferson and their mother and father came up the hill.

"Look at the poor little old dead possum," Rose Mary said.

When everything was still, the possum slowly got to his feet and looked around. The river was crowding up the slope of the hill. A log floated past—maybe his own log. A boat went by and it was full of people. He saw a table floating on the water.

Far ahead were people on their way to the top of the hill, and some drove cows before them, and others led horses—

At the top of the hill, a soldier spoke to Mr. Jackson. "We have a tent for you," he said. "And there's plenty of hot food ready."

Rose Mary and Jefferson and their parents stood in line for food and for warm gray blankets. And afterward, they went into their tent and lay down on the earth to sleep.

"Wrapped in that blanket, you look like a gray log," Jefferson said.

But Rose Mary didn't hear, for she was asleep.

Night came, and the possum felt his way through the grasses with his whiskers. When he finally reached the top of the dark hill, he was hungry and tired. He looked in the first tent, and he thought he saw four gray logs lying on the ground.

He sniffed the nearest. He smelled an enemy.

Rose Mary sat up. "Papa," she said. "Papa. I heard something."

Her father snapped on a flashlight. "I don't see anything," he said.

"There's another little dead possum," she said.

"Maybe it's not dead," Jefferson said. "Maybe it's only pretending. They do, you know."

"He's an ugly fellow," her father said.

"I think he's nice-looking, for a possum," Rose Mary said. She sat down beside him and touched his rough fur. "He feels cold. He feels dead."

"Put something to eat in front of his nose and see what happens," Jefferson said.

"There are some berries in the basket," his mother said.

Rose Mary put the berries on the ground close to the possum's pointed nose.

The possum lay for a long time as though he were dead, and he hardly dared breathe, he was so frightened. Then he smelled something so good that he had to get up and look around.

The people didn't move and he was very hungry.

He ate the berries. They were fat and ripe and good. And when he had finished, the father reached out his hand, and the possum was afraid. He knew he had to climb high to be safe. He ran up along Rose Mary's arm, and she didn't move. He sat on her shoulder.

This was better than a tree. He was warm and comfortable. It was almost as good as a hollow log.

"He's getting tame," Rose Mary said. "When we go home, we can take him with us."

And during the days that passed while they waited to go home, planes flew overhead and looked for people and animals who needed help.

Steamboats churned the yellow water and pulled barges loaded with people and animals who had been rescued from the roofs of houses and barns.

Levees were built and made strong to hold the great river. And as time passed, the possum grew tamer. He followed Rose Mary everywhere.

After a while, the river was caught behind the new levees, and it was time for everyone to go back home.

Jefferson and his mother and father and sister started down the hill, and the possum sat on Rose Mary's shoulder all the way to the little brown house near the bottom of the hill.

Then they were home, and there was a mark high on the wall to show that the Mississippi River had risen almost to the ceiling.

The possum found a hollow log near the back door to live in. Sometimes he came out and sat on Rose Mary's shoulder. More often he hunted for mushrooms or mice, and he wasn't afraid—much of the time.

 Reader's Response

Which part of this story seemed most real to you? Why?

Mississippi Possum

Questions

1. Why was the possum afraid of hawks, owls, bobcats, and foxes?
2. What was surprising about a dog and a rabbit, and a fox and a turkey traveling together?
3. In what two ways did the possum protect himself from danger? Explain how you got your answer.
4. How did the possum's life change after the flood?
5. Do you think the people in the story had had floods before? How do you know?

Writing to Learn

THINK AND ANALYZE The setting of a story is its time and place. Draw a picture of the possum in a setting from either the beginning or the end of the story.

WRITE Use your picture to help you write about the setting. Describe the setting that you chose. Be sure to tell how the possum feels.

Cynthia in the Snow

It SUSHES.
It hushes
The loudness in the road.
It flitter-twitters,
And laughs away from me.
It laughs a lovely whiteness,
And whitely whirs away,
To be
Some otherwhere,
Still white as milk or shirts.
So beautiful it hurts.

Gwendolyn Brooks

292

April Rain Song

Let the rain kiss you.
Let the rain beat upon your head with silver
    liquid drops.
Let the rain sing you a lullaby.

The rain makes still pools on the sidewalk.
The rain makes running pools in the gutter.
The rain plays a little sleep-song on our roof
    at night—
And I love the rain.

Langston Hughes

When a terrible drought comes to Kapiti
Plain, Ki-pat feels he has to find a way to end it.

BRINGING THE RAIN

A NANDI TALE
retold by Verna Aardema
illustrated by Beatriz Vidal

This is the great
Kapiti Plain,
All fresh and green
from the African rains—

TO KAPITI PLAIN

A sea of grass for the
   ground birds to nest in,
And patches of shade for
   wild creatures to rest in;
With acacia trees for
   giraffes to browse on,
And grass for the herdsmen
   to pasture their cows on.

But one year the rains
   were so very belated,
That all of the big wild
   creatures migrated.
Then Ki-pat helped to end
   that terrible drought—
And this story tells
   how it all came about!

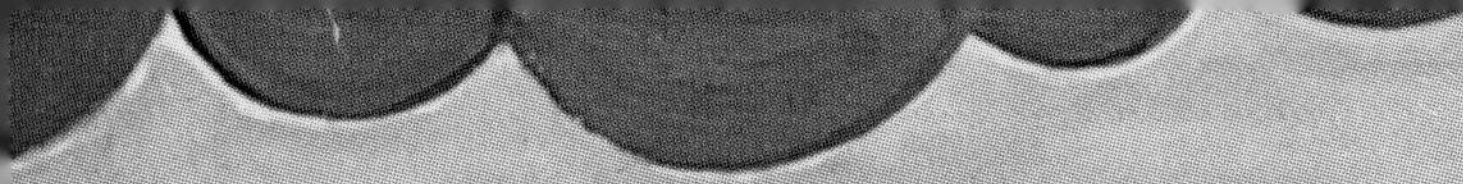

This is the cloud,
all heavy with rain,
That shadowed the ground
on Kapiti Plain.

This is the grass,
all brown and dead,
That needed the rain
from the cloud overhead—
The big, black cloud,
all heavy with rain,
That shadowed the ground
on Kapiti Plain.

These are the cows,
all hungry and dry,
Who mooed for the rain
to fall from the sky;
To green-up the grass,
all brown and dead,
That needed the rain
from the cloud overhead—
The big, black cloud,
all heavy with rain,
That shadowed the ground
on Kapiti Plain.

This is Ki-pat,
  who watched his herd
As he stood on one leg,
  like the big stork bird;
Ki-pat, whose cows
  were so hungry and dry,
They mooed for the rain
  to fall from the sky;
To green-up the grass,
  all brown and dead,
That needed the rain
  from the cloud overhead—
The big, black cloud,
  all heavy with rain,
That shadowed the ground
  on Kapiti Plain.

This is the eagle
  who dropped a feather,
A feather that helped
  to change the weather.
It fell near Ki-pat,
  who watched his herd
As he stood on one leg,
  like the big stork bird;
Ki-pat, whose cows
  were so hungry and dry,
They mooed for the rain
  to fall from the sky;
To green-up the grass,
  all brown and dead,
That needed the rain
  from the cloud overhead—
The big, black cloud,
  all heavy with rain,
That shadowed the ground
  on Kapiti Plain.

This is the arrow
  Ki-pat put together,
With a slender stick
  and an eagle feather;
From the eagle who happened
  to drop a feather,
A feather that helped
  to change the weather.

It fell near Ki-pat,
  who watched his herd
As he stood on one leg,
  like the big stork bird;
Ki-pat, whose cows
  were so hungry and dry,
They mooed for the rain
  to fall from the sky;
To green-up the grass,
  all brown and dead,
That needed the rain
  from the cloud overhead—
The big, black cloud,
  all heavy with rain,
That shadowed the ground
  on Kapiti Plain.

This is the bow,
    so long and strong,
And strung with a string,
    a leather thong;
A bow for the arrow
    Ki-pat put together,
With a slender stick
    and an eagle feather;
From the eagle who happened
    to drop a feather,
A feather that helped
    to change the weather.

It fell near Ki-pat,
    who watched his herd
As he stood on one leg,
    like the big stork bird;
Ki-pat, whose cows
    were so hungry and dry,
They mooed for the rain
    to fall from the sky;
To green-up the grass,
    all brown and dead,
That needed the rain
    from the cloud overhead—
The big, black cloud,
    all heavy with rain,
That shadowed the ground
    on Kapiti Plain.

This was the shot
 that pierced the cloud
And loosed the rain
 with thunder LOUD!
A shot from the bow,
 so long and strong,
And strung with a string,
 a leather thong;
A bow for the arrow
 Ki-pat put together,
With a slender stick
 and an eagle feather;
From the eagle who happened
 to drop a feather,
A feather that helped
 to change the weather.

It fell near Ki-pat,
     who watched his herd
As he stood on one leg,
     like the big stork bird;
Ki-pat, whose cows
     were so hungry and dry,
They mooed for the rain
     to fall from the sky;
To green-up the grass,
     all brown and dead,
That needed the rain
     from the cloud overhead—
The big, black cloud,
     all heavy with rain,
That shadowed the ground
     on Kapiti Plain.

So the grass grew green,
     and the cattle fat!
And Ki-pat got a wife
     and a little Ki-pat—

Who tends the cows now,
     and shoots down the rain,
When black clouds shadow
     Kapiti Plain.

 Reader's **Response**

    What words would you use to describe
Ki-pat?

BRINGING THE RAIN
TO KAPITI PLAIN

Questions

1. In what ways was the Kapiti Plain important to the different animals?
2. What went wrong one year?
3. Why do you think Ki-pat felt he had to do something?
4. What steps did Ki-pat take to make the bow and arrow? Tell how you figured out each step.
5. What might have happened if Ki-pat had not brought the rain to Kapiti Plain?

Writing to Learn

THINK AND IMAGINE This poem creates beautiful word pictures. Read the poem and look at the picture the poem suggests.

This is the cloud
   all heavy with rain,
That shadowed the ground
   on Kapiti Plain.

WRITE Look outside your classroom window. Write a sentence that tells about one thing you see. Make your sentence a word picture of what you see.

READING FICTION

Literature:
Tall Tales

Imagine a man so big that his footsteps created the Great Lakes! What do you think of an ox that measured 746 ax handles from one eye to the other? These characters exist—not in real life, but in tall tales. Tall tales are funny stories about folk characters such as Paul Bunyan, John Henry, Pecos Bill, and Slue-Foot Sue. Many of these American heroes were made up in people's imaginations. Others are based on real people, such as Annie Oakley and Davy Crockett.

Tall tales may once have had a grain of truth in them. Over the years, though, the truth became more and more exaggerated and unbelievable. Woodcutters, cowboys, and other people who lived in the old West made each other laugh by making up tall tales about the adventures of their favorite characters.

Tall Tales Are Super Fun

Often tall tales included funny explanations of how real things, such as the Grand Canyon or the Mississippi River, came to be. You've probably heard of Paul Bunyan, the giant woodcutter who was taller than the tallest pine tree. Paul dug out Puget Sound, a large body of water in the state of Washington. It was easy. He used an enormous shovel! Then he and his great blue ox, Babe, hauled the dirt a few miles away. They piled it up to create Mt. Rainier.

Other tall-tale heroes did amazing things, too. Pecos Bill, the cowboy hero of the West, once rode a tornado. John Henry was the "steel-drivin' " man who helped to build railroads in the South. He beat a machine in a race to see which of them could dig through solid rock faster. In one story, Slue-Foot Sue rode a catfish as big as a whale down the Rio Grande. Imagine what a ride that must have been!

Tall tales are fun to read because the characters in the tales do unexpected things. Instead of climbing a mountain, Paul Bunyan builds one. Most people would run from a tornado, but not Pecos Bill—he rides one. The actions of the characters in tall tales surprise and entertain us.

Read and Enjoy

The next story you will read is a tall tale about Pecos Bill and Slue-Foot Sue. As you read it, open your imagination to the entertaining deeds you will read about.

Lack of rain was a problem on Kapiti Plain. It can also be a problem in other parts of the world. Luckily for the folks in Texas, Slue-Foot Sue and her husband, Pecos Bill, are there to help out.

Pecos Bill
and Slue-Foot Sue, the Rainmaker

by Elizabeth and Carl Carmer

Pecos Bill was a very famous cowboy. So famous that other cowboys used to talk about him. "Pecos Bill," they said, "can throw a loop farther than any cowboy. He can lasso a dozen cows safely in a single bundle. Pecos Bill is the greatest cowboy in the West."

Pecos Bill broke many wild horses to the saddle. His favorite was a mustang called Widow-Maker. Other cowboys had tried to tame Widow-Maker but they failed. The horse had bucked and twisted so much that they were thrown off his back. Sometimes they were hurt badly. Only Pecos Bill could ride Widow-Maker.

Late one clear night, Bill rode Widow-Maker along the Pecos River. Thousands of stars were mirrored in the stream. Bill felt lonely. Then a round moon rose. It made the night as clear as day.

Bill saw a sight he would never forget. Down the shining river came a pretty girl riding bareback on a Texas catfish. The catfish was rearing and plunging and bucking. But the girl was riding him smoothly and easily. When she saw Bill, she edged the fish close to the river bank.

"My name is Slue-Foot Sue," she said. "I am the champion girl rider in all the West."

"You are very pretty, too," said Bill.

"I like being a good rider better than being pretty," said Sue.

That afternoon Bill and Sue sat and talked. By the end of the day they had decided to get married.

Folks came from miles around to the big wedding party the next week. For wedding gifts all the guests gave Bill and Sue lassos.

Slue-Foot Sue and Pecos Bill lived happily for a few months at their ranch beside the Pecos River. But no rains came in the spring. The yellow waters of the Pecos began to dry up. Not a drop of water fell from the sky. Sue had to keep her catfish in the old swimming hole. The rest of the river was too shallow for him to swim in. Widow-Maker galloped up the mountain every day. He drank the cold water from the melting snow near the top.

One night, all the Texas stars looked as if they had been cleaned and polished.

"Bill," Sue said to her husband. "Do we still have all those lassos we got for wedding presents?"

"They're in the woodshed," said Pecos Bill.

"Please get them," said Slue-Foot Sue. "I want you to tie them all together and make the longest lasso in the world. We are going to climb the mountain and I want you to bring the lasso along."

Bill looked puzzled.

At the top of the mountain the stars looked even nearer and brighter than before.

Sue asked, "Do you see the Little Dipper?"

"Yes," said Bill.

"Can you throw our lasso over the handle?" asked Sue. "Then if we both pull hard enough we might tip the dipper. The water inside would pour out."

"A good idea!" shouted Bill. "I can rope it. Just give me room to get the loop started!"

311

Soon the lasso was circling Bill's head. It made a singing sound through the bright air. Bill kept adding more rope to its length. At last, with one great toss, Bill let it go. Up, up it went toward the stars of the Little Dipper. Sue and Bill waited. It seemed a long time before the line suddenly tightened.

"I've got it," shouted Bill. "Now pull."

Pull they did, as hard as they could. Slowly the handle of the Little Dipper began to turn. Bill and Sue pulled even harder and the handle moved a little more. All night they tugged and tugged at the long rope.

Finally Sue said, "The Little Dipper's tipped enough. The water must be spilling. Let's tie the lasso fast and go home."

Daylight had begun to appear. Then suddenly there came a splatter of raindrops as big as oranges. Soon a steady stream of rain poured from the Dipper.

Bill and Sue walked home wet and happy. The falling rain washed the dusty brown trees and turned them green. The shining Pecos River overflowed its banks. Widow-Maker was drinking from it. Sue's catfish swam about joyfully.

Suddenly the rays of the rising sun struck the falling water. The biggest rainbow ever seen anywhere arched across the Texas sky.

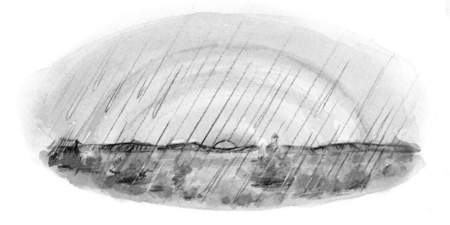

◆ LIBRARY LINK ◆

If you enjoyed reading this tall tale, you might enjoy Pecos Bill Rides a Tornado, *retold by Wyatt Blassingame.*

Reader's Response

Which parts of this tall tale did you find the funniest?

Writing a Description

In this unit people reacted to weather in different ways. When no rain came, Slue-Foot Sue and Pecos Bill tipped the Little Dipper to bring rain to the dry earth. Ki-pat shot an arrow through a cloud to bring rain to Kapiti Plain.

We respond to weather in different ways, too. Can you remember a day when the weather surprised or pleased you?

Write a description of the weather on that day.

Prewriting

Read the "weather words" in the box. Choose words from the box that will help you describe the weather on this day.

────────────── Weather Words ──────────────

Sunny	Rainy
hot bright burning heat	wet slippery pouring rain
Windy	**Snowy**
blowing gusting howling winds	sparkling snowdrifts snowflakes

Writing

Write your description of what happened on the weather day. Write a topic sentence that tells what the weather was like. Next add detail sentences that tell about the weather. Describe what you saw, heard, felt, smelled, and tasted. Be sure to use words from your box of weather words.

Revising

Put your writing away for a while. Later, read it again carefully. Have you used descriptive words such as *icy cold* or *gusting winds* to help your readers "feel" the weather on your special day?

Proofreading

Use a dictionary to check your spelling. Make sure you used capitalization correctly. Then copy your paragraph neatly on a sheet of paper.

Publishing

Share your description with your classmates. Then put all the descriptions together to make a book about weather. Choose a title for the book.

WORKING TOGETHER

Describing the Weather

The stories in this unit showed how weather affects people and animals. For example, in the story "Mississippi Possum," the Jeffersons had to leave their home when the river flooded.

Your group will write the radio weather report that the Jeffersons heard just before they had to leave their home. Plan your weather report together.

As you work, help make sure your group does these things:

◆ Listen when others talk.

◆ Finish on time.

◆ Encourage others to share ideas.

◆ Make a list of the group's ideas.

Together, plan and write the radio weather report. One member of the group can be the director. One can make sound effects to suggest the weather. One student can think of music for the report. One student can read the report aloud.

Practice presenting the report. When you are ready, share the report with the rest of the class.

Cloudy with a Chance of Meatballs by Judi Barrett *(Macmillan, 1978)* In the town of Chewandswallow, it snows mashed potatoes, blows storms of hamburgers, and rains juice and soup.

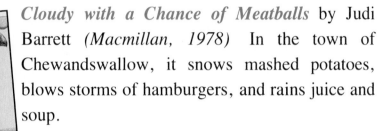

From the Hills of Georgia: An Autobiography in Paintings by Mattie Lou O'Kelley *(Little, Brown, 1983)* This story tells of growing up on a farm in Georgia at the beginning of this century.

Island Winter by Charles Martin *(Greenwillow, 1986)* Heather wonders how she will pass the time on an island off the coast of New England after the summer crowds have left. She discovers that each season brings its own special events.

First Snow by Helen Coutant, illustrated by Vo-Dinh *(Knopf, 1974)* A Vietnamese family's first experience with snow is filled with joy and sadness when the grandmother dies.

BROWSING FOR BOOKS

And on This Shelf We Have . . .

By now you have probably discovered that libraries are very much like supermarkets. In the supermarket each kind of food has its own special section. When you know just where to find cereals or ice cream or fruit juices, it's easy, and fun, to go looking for your favorite kind.

In the library, different kinds of books also have their own special sections. You probably wouldn't have any trouble going right to the table that has those large picture books you liked before you could read. By now you have probably found some other kinds of books and can even picture where you went to get them. There was that book about caring for cats that you needed when someone gave you a new kitten. Or there was the mystery story that your friend said you should read.

Your library has many kinds of books, and they are waiting for you to discover them. Reading a book of fairy tales might be a wonderful way to spend part of the weekend. Or, you might like a book about a real person, like Abraham Lincoln, Martin Luther King, Jr., Amelia Earhart, or Babe Ruth. Those are only some of the many kinds of books you'll find by browsing in your library. Take an hour to browse. It could be the best hour you'll spend all week.

The Wreck of the
Zephyr

written and illustrated by
CHRIS VAN ALLSBURG

Once, while traveling along the seashore, I stopped at a small fishing village. After eating lunch, I decided to take a walk. I followed a path out of the village, uphill to some cliffs high above the sea. At the edge of these cliffs was a most unusual sight—the wreck of a small sailboat.

An old man was sitting among the broken timbers, smoking a pipe. He seemed to be reading my mind when he said, "Odd, isn't it?"

"Yes," I answered. "How did it get here?"

"Waves carried it up during a storm."

"Really?" I said. "It doesn't seem the waves could ever get that high."

The old man smiled. "Well, there is another story." He invited me to have a seat and listen to his strange tale.

"In our village, years ago," he said, "there was a boy who could sail a boat better than any man in the harbor. He could find a breeze over the flattest sea. When dark clouds kept other boats at anchor, the boy would sail out, ready to prove to the villagers, to the sea itself, how great a sailor he was.

"One morning, under an ominous sky, he prepared to take his boat, the *Zephyr*, out to sea. A fisherman warned the boy to stay in port. Already a strong wind was blowing. 'I'm not afraid,' the boy said, 'because I'm the greatest sailor there is.' The fisherman pointed to a sea gull gliding overhead. 'There's the only sailor who can go out on a day like this.' The boy just laughed as he hoisted his sails into a blustery wind.

"The wind whistled in the rigging as the *Zephyr* pounded her way through the water. The sky grew black and the waves rose up like mountains. The boy struggled to keep his boat from going over. Suddenly a gust of wind caught the sail. The boom swung around and hit the boy's head. He fell to the cockpit floor and did not move.

"When the boy opened his eyes, he found himself lying on a beach. The *Zephyr* rested behind him, carried there by the storm. The boat was far from the water's edge. The tide would not carry it back to sea. The boy set out to look for help.

"He walked for a long time and was surprised that he didn't recognize the shoreline. He climbed a hill, expecting to see something familiar, but what he saw instead was a strange and unbelievable sight. Before him were two boats, sailing high above the water. Astonished, he watched them glide by. Then a third sailed past, towing the *Zephyr*. The boats entered a bay that was bordered by a large village. There they left the *Zephyr*.

"The boy made his way down to the harbor, to the dock where the boat was tied. He met a sailor who smiled when he saw the boy. Pointing to the *Zephyr* he asked, 'Yours?' The boy nodded. The sailor said they almost never saw strangers on their island. It was surrounded by a treacherous reef. The *Zephyr* must have been carried over the reef by the storm. He told the boy that, later, they would take him and the *Zephyr* back over the reef. But the boy said he would not leave until he learned to sail above the waves. The sailor told him it took years to learn to sail like that. 'Besides,' he said, 'the *Zephyr* does not have the right sails.' The boy insisted. He pleaded with the sailor.

"Finally the sailor said he would try to teach him if the boy promised to leave the next morning. The boy agreed. The sailor went to a shed and got a new set of sails.

"All afternoon they sailed back and forth across the bay. Sometimes the sailor took the tiller, and the boat would magically begin to lift out of the water. But when the boy tried, he could not catch the wind that made boats fly.

"When the sun went down they went back to the harbor. They dropped anchor and a fisherman rowed them to shore. 'In the morning,' the sailor said, 'we'll put your own sails back on the *Zephyr* and send you home.' He took the boy to his house, and the sailor's wife fed them oyster stew.

333

"After dinner the sailor played the concertina. He sang a song about a man named Samuel Blue, who, long ago, tried to sail his boat over land and crashed:

For the wind o'er land's ne'er steady nor true,
an' all men that sail there'll meet Samuel Blue.

"When he was done with his song, the sailor sent the boy to bed. But the boy could not sleep. He knew he could fly his boat if he had another chance. He waited until the sailor and his wife were asleep, then he quietly dressed and went to the harbor. As he rowed out to the *Zephyr*, the boy felt the light evening wind grow stronger and colder.

335

"Under a full moon, he sailed the *Zephyr* into the bay. He tried to remember everything the sailor had told him. He tried to feel the wind pulling his boat forward, lifting it up. Then, suddenly, the boy felt the *Zephyr* begin to shake. The sound of the water rushing past the hull grew louder. The air filled with spray as the boat sliced through the waves. The bow slowly began to lift. Higher and higher the *Zephyr* rose out of the water, then finally broke free. The sound of rushing water stopped. There was only the sound of wind in the sails. The *Zephyr* was flying.

"Using the stars to guide him, the boy set a course for home. The wind blew very hard, churning the sea below. But that did not matter to the *Zephyr* as she glided through the night sky. When clouds blocked the boy's view of the stars, he trimmed the sails and climbed higher. Surely the men of the island never dared fly so high. Now the boy was certain he was truly the greatest sailor of all.

"He steered well. Before the night was over, he saw the moonlit spire of the church at the edge of his village. As he drew closer to land, an idea took hold of him. He would sail over the village and ring the *Zephyr*'s bell. Then everyone would see him and know that he was the greatest sailor. He flew over the tree-topped cliffs of the shore, but as he reached the church the *Zephyr* began to fall.

"The wind had shifted. The boy pulled as hard as he could on the tiller, but it did no good. The wind shifted again. He steered for the open sea, but the trees at the cliff's edge stood between him and the water. At first there was just the rustle of leaves brushing the hull. Then the air was filled with the sound of breaking branches and ripping sails. The boat fell to the ground. And here she sits today."

341

"A remarkable tale," I said, as the old man stopped to relight his pipe. "What happened to the boy?"

"He broke his leg that night. Of course, no one believed his story about flying boats. It was easier for them to believe that he was lost in the storm and thrown up here by the waves." The old man laughed.

"No sir, the boy never amounted to much. People thought he was crazy. He just took odd jobs around the harbor. Most of the time he was out sailing, searching for that island and a new set of sails."

A light breeze blew through the trees. The old man looked up. "Wind coming," he said. "I've got some sailing to do." He picked up a cane, and I watched as he limped slowly toward the harbor.

343

GLOSSARY

Full pronunciation key*   The pronunciation of each word is shown just after the word, in this way: **abbreviate** (ə brē′vē āt).

The letters and signs used are pronounced as in the words below.

The mark **′** is placed after a syllable with a primary or heavy accent as in the example above.

The mark **′** after a syllable shows a secondary or lighter accent, as in **abbreviation** (ə brē′vē ā′shən).

SYMBOL	KEY WORDS	SYMBOL	KEY WORDS	SYMBOL	KEY WORDS
a	ask, fat	u	up, cut	r	red, dear
ā	ape, date	ʉr	fur, fern	s	sell, pass
ä	car, father			t	top, hat
		ə	a in ago	v	vat, have
e	elf, ten		e in agent	w	will, always
er	berry, care		e in father	y	yet, yard
ē	even, meet		i in unity	z	zebra, haze
			o in collect		
i	is, hit		u in focus	ch	chin, arch
ir	mirror, here			ŋ̂	ring, singer
ī	ice, fire	b	bed, dub	sh	she, dash
		d	did, had	th	thin, truth
o	lot, pond	f	fall, off	*th*	then, father
ō	open, go	g	get, dog	zh	s in pleasure
ô	law, horn	h	he, ahead		
ɔi	oil, point	j	joy, jump	′	as in (ā′b′l)
o͞o	look, pull	k	kill, bake		
o͞o	ooze, tool	l	let, ball		
yo͞o	unite, cure	m	met, trim		
yo͞o	cute, few	n	not, ton		
ɔu	out, crowd	p	put, tap		

*Pronunciation key and respellings adapted from *Webster's New World Dictionary, Basic School Edition,* Copyright © 1983 by Simon & Schuster, Inc. Reprinted by permission.

A

a·ca·cia tree (ə kā′shə trē′) *noun.* a tall shrub that grows in warm parts of the world. It has feathery leaves and bunches of yellow or white flowers. **acacia trees.**

ad·mire (əd mīr′) *verb.* to think of someone or something with approval and respect: Everyone *admired* the painting at the museum. **admired.**

ad·vis·er or **ad·vis·or** (əd vīz′ər) *noun.* a person who gives ideas to others, often used by leaders of countries or businesses to help solve problems. **advisers, advisors.**

a·larm (ə lärm′) *noun.* **1.** a warning of danger given by shouting, ringing bells, etc. **2.** a sudden call to fight. **3.** fear that is caused by danger.

a·lert (ə lurt′) *verb.* to warn people to be ready for possible danger.

an·e·mom·e·ter (an′ə mom′ə tər) *noun.* an instrument used to measure how fast the wind is blowing.

an·i·mal groom·er (an′ə m′l grōōm′ər) *noun.* a person who is paid to take special care of animals, such as brushing hair, clipping nails, etc.: The *animal groomer* carefully cut the poodle's hair.

an·nals (an″lz) *plural noun.* **1.** records of important things written down year by year in the order they happened. **2.** historical records.

anx·ious·ly (angk′shəs lē) *adverb.* **1.** in an uneasy or worried way. **2.** wishing eagerly.

arch (ärch) *noun.* **1.** a curve-shaped line, like those found on the fingertips. **2.** anything shaped like an arch, such as doors, windows, bridges, etc. **arches.**

as·sign (ə sīn′) *verb.* **1.** to give out a task or job: The teacher *assigned* us a book report. **2.** to set aside for a special reason or purpose. **assigned.**

as·sist·ant (ə sis′tənt) *noun.* someone who assists or helps another person; helper.

at·las (at′ləs) *noun.* a book of maps.

acacia tree

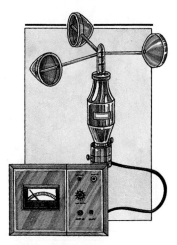
anemometer

◇

Atlas was the name given to a book of maps because such books often had a picture of Atlas, the Greek god who held the world on his shoulders.

atlas

bamboo

baobab

barge

at·mos·phere (at′məs fir) *noun.* **1.** all the air around the earth: The earth's *atmosphere* is made up of different gases. **2.** the air in a place. **3.** the general feeling or mood of a place or thing.

at·om (at′əm) *noun.* **1.** the smallest bits of matter that join together to form all objects, gases, etc.: Everything in the universe is made up of *atoms.* **2.** a small piece or part of anything. **atoms.**

at·tach (ə tach′) *verb.* **1.** to fasten or join together as by tying or sticking; to connect. **2.** to bring close by feelings of love. **3.** to add to the end of something.

a·ward (ə wôrd′) *noun.* a prize given for excellence or in recognition of some achievement. **awards.**

B

bal·ance (bal′əns) *noun.* **1.** an instrument or tool for weighing things. **2.** a state in which two things are equal in weight, amount, etc.

bam·boo (bam boo′) *noun.* tall grass that grows like a tree in hot, or tropical, regions of the world. The hollow, woody stems are used in making window blinds, canes, fishing poles, and other things. **bamboos.**

ban·dage (ban′dij) *noun.* a strip or piece of cloth used to cover a sore, cut, or wound.

ba·o·bab (bā′ō bab′) *noun.* a tree with a wide trunk that grows in parts of Africa and India. **baobabs.**

barge (bärj) *noun.* a large boat with a flat bottom, used to carry heavy things on rivers and canals: The *barge* stopped at many places along the river to pick up different kinds of goods.

ba·ton (bə ton′) *noun.* **1.** a thin stick used by the leader of an orchestra, band, or chorus to direct the group. **2.** a large stick twirled by a drum major or majorette.

beast (bēst) *noun.* any large animal that has four feet: The campers were awakened by a *beast* searching for food.

be·lat·ed (bi lāt′id) *adjective.* too late; not on time: He sent a *belated* birthday card to his friend.

bi·cus·pid (bī kus′pid) *noun.* a tooth that has two points on the top.

bind (bīnd) *verb.* **1.** to tie together with rope or cloth; to tie tightly. **2.** to wrap a bandage around something. **3.** to keep together because of strong feelings, beliefs, or promises.

bin·oc·u·lars (bi nok′yə lərz) *plural noun.* two small telescopes that are fastened together. When looked through with both eyes, they make distant things seem closer and larger.

bird of par·a·dise (bʉrd uv par′ə dīs) *noun.* **1.** any of a number of brightly colored birds from New Guinea. **2.** a plant from Africa with large, pointed flowers resembling a bird's beak.

blimp (blimp) *noun.* a lighter-than-air airship shaped like an egg, used to carry people or things.

blood ves·sel (blud′ ves″l) *noun.* one of many tubes in the body through which blood flows: Arteries, veins, and capillaries are *blood vessels.* **blood vessels.**

boast (bōst) *verb.* to talk about what you have or what you have done with too much pride; to brag: We were tired of the way he *boasted* about winning the medal. **boasted.**

both·er (both′er) *verb.* **1.** to cause trouble or worry; annoy: We were *bothered* by all the noise in the gym. **2.** to take the time or trouble to do something. **bothered.**

bought (bôt) *verb. the past tense and past participle of* **buy.** to have received something by paying money for it: He *bought* the game at the toy store.

bridge (brij) *noun.* **1.** the thin, curved piece of a violin over which strings are stretched. **2.** something built across a river, railroad tracks, etc., so that people or cars can cross over from one side to the other. **3.** the upper, bony part of the human nose. **4.** a platform above the main deck of a ship, from which the ship is controlled.

browse (brouz) *verb.* **1.** to nibble at leaves, twigs, or grass: Giraffes often *browse* in tall trees. **2.** to look through a book, stopping to read different parts. **3.** to go slowly through a place or look over things.

a fat	oi oil	ch chin
ā ape	oo look	sh she
ä car, father	o͞o tool	th thin
e ten	ou out	*th* then
er care	u up	zh leisure
ē even	ur fur	n̂g ring
i hit		
ir here	ə = a *in* ago	
ī bite, fire	e *in* agent	
o lot	i *in* unity	
ō go	o *in* collect	
ô law, horn	u *in* focus	

binoculars

Blimp got its name from a type of aircraft called a *limp.* Limps were soft unless they were filled with the gas that made them lighter than air. There were two types of limps: A and B. The B limp was the most common. Soon its name was changed to blimp.

C

calculator

Ceilometer is a word made up of two words from Latin. *Ceil* means "sky" and *meter* means "measured." So a *ceilometer* is an instrument that measures the height of the clouds. The suffix *-meter* usually shows that the word is about measurement.

cal·a·bash (kal′ə bash) *noun.*
1. a tree, found in tropical areas, having a fruit that looks like a gourd. **2.** a bowl or other container made of the dried, hollow shell of a fruit that looks like a gourd.

cal·cu·la·tor (kal′kyə lāt′ər) *noun.* a machine that does arithmetic quickly.

car·pen·ter (kär′pən tər) *noun.* a person who builds or repairs things made of wood.

cat·a·logue or **cat·a·log** (kat″l ôg) *noun.* **1.** a printed list or book with pictures and descriptions of things for sale: We looked through several *catalogues,* but we could not find the boots we wanted. **2.** a file of cards in alphabetical order that is a complete list of things, such as all the books in a library. **catalogues** or **catalogs.**

ceil·om·e·ter (sē lom′ə tər) *noun.* an instrument that measures the height of clouds above the ground.

chant (chant) *verb.* to talk in a sing-song way, sometimes over and over. —*noun.* a song with many words sung in the same tone.

char·ac·ter (kar′ik tər) *noun.*
1. someone in a story or play: The prince and princess are the main *characters* in the fairy tale. **2.** a person's thoughts, feelings, and actions; what a person is like. **3.** any letter, number, or symbol that is used in writing or printing, or in a computer. **characters.**

char·ac·ter·is·tic (kar′ik tər is′tik) *noun.* a special feature, trait, or quality of a person or thing: Her best *characteristics* are her love of life and her sense of humor. **characteristics.**

cher·ish (cher′ish) *verb.* to treat someone or something with love and care; take care of; treasure. **cherishes.**

chor·tle (chôr′t′l) *verb.* to laugh; to make a gleeful chuckle. **chortled.**

chuck·le (chuk″l) *verb.* to laugh softly. **chuckled.**

churn (churn) *verb.* **1.** to move or stir around with great force: The wind *churned* the leaves around the field. **2.** to beat cream until it turns to butter. **churned.**

clar·i·net (klar ə net′) *noun.* a woodwind musical instrument that is played by blowing into a mouthpiece while covering holes in the long body with the fingertips or with keys.

cla·vier (klə vir′) *noun.* any instrument having strings and a keyboard, such as the piano or harpsichord.

cloak (klōk) *noun.* **1.** a loose piece of outer clothing, usually having no sleeves. **2.** something that covers or hides.

cock·a·too (kok′ə tōō) *noun.* a parrot with a crest on its head and white feathers colored in places with pink and yellow. **cockatoos.**

col·o·nist (kol′ə nist) *noun.* a person who, with others, settles in another land, far from his or her home country: Early *colonists* from Europe were helped by the Native Americans in North America. **colonists.**

com·pose (kəm pōz′) *verb.* **1.** to write or create, especially music: He *composed* a beautiful song. **2.** to make by mixing two or more things together. **composed.**

com·pos·er (kəm pō′zər) *noun.* a person who composes, especially one who writes music.

com·put·er (kəm pyōōt′ər) *noun.* a machine that can store, work with, and give back information.

con·cert (kon′sərt) *noun.* a program of music in which musicians play together.

con·duc·tor (kən duk′tər) *noun.* **1.** a person who directs an orchestra: Everyone applauded when the *conductor* came on stage. **2.** the person who collects tickets or money on a train.

con·ser·va·to·ry (kən sur′və tor′ē) *noun.* **1.** a room, enclosed in glass, for growing and showing plants; a small greenhouse. **2.** a school of music, art, etc.

con·stant (kon′stənt) *adjective.* **1.** always the same; unchanging. **2.** loyal or faithful.

con·test (kon′test) *noun.* **1.** a race, game, etc., in which each person or team tries to win. **2.** a struggle or fight.

cour·ti·er (kôr′tē ər) *noun.* a person present at a royal palace or court; an attendant. **courtiers.**

cre·ate (krē āt′) *verb.* **1.** to make something for the first time: We watched as the artist *created* a beautiful statue. **2.** to cause or make happen. **created, creating.**

a fat	oi oil	ch chin
ā ape	oo look	sh she
ä car, father	ōō tool	th thin
e ten	ou out	*th* then
er care	u up	zh leisure
ē even	ur fur	n̂g ring
i hit		
ir here	ə = a *in* ago	
ī bite, fire	e *in* agent	
o lot	i *in* unity	
ō go	o *in* collect	
ô law, horn	u *in* focus	

cockatoo

Cockatoo comes from Malaysia, a country in the South Pacific. There, they call this type of noisy parrot *kakatuwa*, or "old big sister."

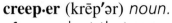

creeper

creep·er (krēp′ər) *noun.*
1. any plant that grows along the ground or a wall and whose stem puts out threadlike parts that hold it in place. **2.** a person or thing that moves along with the body close to the ground.

criss·cross (kris′krôs) *verb.*
1. to move back and forth across. **2.** to mark or make a pattern of crossing lines.

cure (kyoor) *verb.* to make a sick person well; to return to good health: The doctor *cured* my sore throat. **cured.**

crisscross

D

de·fense·less (di fens′lis) *adjective.* being helpless; not able to protect oneself.

del·i·cate (del′i kit) *adjective.*
1. slight and not easily felt: The child used a *delicate* touch when she picked up the flowers. **2.** light, mild, or soft; not strong. **3.** very finely made. **4.** easily spoiled or broken.

del·i·ca·tes·sen (del′i kə tes″n) *noun.* a store that sells foods that are ready to eat, such as cheeses, cooked meats, salads, etc.

delicate

de·light·ful (di līt′fəl) *adjective.* very pleasing; giving great pleasure or delight.

den·tine (den′tēn) *noun.* the hard, bony material forming the main part of a tooth.

de·scend·ant (di sen′dənt) *noun.* a person who is related by birth to someone, or some family, who lived many years before. **descendants.**

dig·ni·ty (dig′nə tē) *noun.*
1. pride or self-respect: She accepted the award with great *dignity.* **2.** the condition of being worthy of respect.

dis·may (dis mā′) *noun.*
1. alarm or shock; great fear. **2.** a loss of courage when faced with a problem or danger.

drought (drout) *noun.* a long period of time when there is little or no rain. **droughts.**

E

earn (urn) *verb.* **1.** to be paid for work that is done: She *earns* money for walking her neighbor's dog. **2.** to get or deserve because of something you have done. **earns.**

e·mo·tion·al·ly (i mō′shən′l ē)
adverb. in a way that shows
strong or deep feelings.

en·tire (in tīr′) *adjective.*
having no missing parts;
complete or whole.

es·cape (ə skāp′) *verb.* **1.** to
get free or break loose. **2.** to
avoid harm or getting hurt.
3. to leak out.

es·say (es′ā) *noun.* a short
written piece giving the
author's opinions about
some subject.

e·val·u·ate (i val′yoo wāt) *verb.*
1. to use information to
make a judgment. **2.** to find
out what something is
worth. **evaluating.**

e·ven·tu·al·ly (i ven′choo wəl ē)
adverb. finally; in the end:
All the leaves *eventually* fell
from the tree.

ex·act (ig zakt′) *adjective.*
1. correct to the smallest
detail: My *exact* height is 5
feet, 5¼ inches. **2.** having no
mistakes.

ex·pe·ri·ence (ik spir′ē əns)
noun. **1.** anything that has
happened to a person:
Getting lost in the forest
and seeing a bear were
frightening *experiences.*
2. skill that is gained
through training and
practice. **experiences.**

ex·plo·sion (ik splō′zhən)
noun. **1.** an outburst,
especially of noise or color:
The *explosion* of fireworks
was beautiful to watch. **2.** a
fast or sudden increase in
something.

ex·pres·sion (ik spresh′ən)
noun. **1.** a look that shows
what one feels or means.
2. the act of putting
something into words. **3.** a
certain way of speaking,
reading, singing, etc., that is
persuasive, graceful, gives
meaning, etc. **4.** a common
word or saying. **expressions.**

ex·traor·di·nar·y
(ik strôr′d′n er′ē) *adjective.*
very different from what is
usual; remarkable; very
unusual.

a fat	**oi** oil	**ch** chin
ā ape	**oo** look	**sh** she
ä car, father	**ōo** tool	**th** thin
e ten	**ou** out	**th** then
er care	**u** up	**zh** leisure
ē even	**ur** fur	**ng** ring
i hit		
ir here	**ə** = a *in* ago	
ī bite, fire		e *in* agent
o lot		i *in* unity
ō go		o *in* collect
ô law, horn		u *in* focus

Extraordinary is made up of
two words, *extra* and
ordinary. Sometimes *extra*
means "more than usual." In
this case, *extra* means "on the
outside." So *extraordinary*
means "something outside of
the ordinary" or "something
very special."

F

fan·tas·tic (fan tas′tik)
adjective. **1.** very strange,
unreal, or unbelievable.
2. existing only in the
imagination.

fig·ure·head (fig′yər hed)
noun. **1.** a carved wooden
figure placed on the front of
a ship for decoration. **2.** a
person who seems important
but who has no real power.
figureheads.

figurehead

351

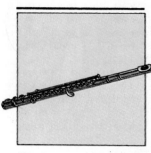
flute

frangipani

groceries

flam·boy·ant (flam boi′ənt) *adjective.* **1.** very colorful and fancy. **2.** too showy or fancy.

flute (floōt) *noun.* a musical wind instrument. It is played by blowing across a mouthpiece while covering different holes along the side with the fingers.

fore·cast (fôr′kast) *verb.* to tell or try to tell what will happen ahead of time; predict: The weather reporter has *forecast* rain for this afternoon.

for·mu·la (fôr′myə lə) *noun.* a set of directions for mixing a medicine, baby's food, etc.

fran·gi·pa·ni (fran′jə pan′ē) *noun.* tropical American shrubs or small trees with large, fragrant flowers.

fu·ri·ous (fyoor′ē əs) *adjective.* full of anger or rage: He was *furious* when his bicycle was broken.

G

gasp (gasp) *verb.* to take a sudden breath because of surprise, shock, or some other strong feeling. **gasped.**

gauge (gāj) *noun.* **1.** an instrument that measures something, such as the amount of water or steam, the thickness of wire, etc. **2.** an agreed-upon measure or scale of measurement.

gen·er·a·tion (jen′ə rā′shən) *noun.* a group of people who are all born and live around the same time and who often have many of the same kinds of experiences: People of his parents' *generation* used to dance to rock 'n' roll music.

gong (gông) *noun.* a round, metal plate that makes a loud, deep ringing sound when struck with a large stick.

good·ie bag (good′ē bag) *noun.* a sack that holds useful things, such as items to help tell a story, or gifts to be handed out.

gown (goun) *noun.* **1.** a long, loose piece of clothing, such as a woman's long dress, usually worn at special times. **2.** a long, loose robe worn by a minister, judge, etc. **gowns.**

gro·cer·ies (grō′sər ēz) *plural noun.* goods such as food and household supplies.

gust (gust) *noun.* a strong, sudden rush of air: A *gust* of wind blew the hat off his head.

H

ham·let (ham′lit) *noun.* a very small village. **hamlets.**

ham·mock (ham′ək) *noun.* a long piece of net or canvas that is hung between two trees and used as a bed or couch.

har·mo·ny (här′mə nē) *noun.*
1. a pleasing arrangement of parts, things, etc.: The flowers in the vase were a *harmony* of colors.
2. musical sounds of different tones played or sung together in a pleasing way.

her·ald (her′əld) *noun.* a person who announces important news.

herds·man (hʉrdz′mən) *noun.* a person who watches over a herd, or group, of animals. **herdsmen.**

hol·low (hol′ō) *adjective.* having an empty space or a hole inside; not solid: The *hollow* log was used to make a canoe.

hoof·beat (hoof′bēt′ *or* hoof′bēt′) *noun.* sound made by any hoofed animal such as a horse when it runs or walks: The villagers heard *hoofbeats* in the distance. **hoofbeats.**

hor·net (hôr′nit) *noun.* a large wasp that lives in a nest and can give a painful sting. **hornets.**

hu·mid·i·ty (hyoo mid′ə tē) *noun.* the amount of water in the air; dampness.

hur·ri·cane (hʉr′ə kān) *noun.* a powerful storm with heavy rain and winds that blow in a circle at 73 or more miles per hour.

hy·grom·e·ter (hī grom′ə tər) *noun.* an instrument used to measure humidity.

I

i·den·ti·fy (ī den′tə fī) *verb.* to show or prove that someone or something is a certain person or thing: He can *identify* that toy car as his own.

i·mag·i·na·tion (i maj′ə nā′shən) *noun.* **1.** the ability to picture things in the mind. **2.** the ability to make up things that are not real or did not really happen.

im·pe·ri·al (im pir′ē əl) *adjective.* having to do with an empire, emperor, or empress; royal.

a fat	oi oil	ch chin
ā ape	oo look	sh she
ä car, father	oo tool	th thin
e ten	ou out	th then
er care	u up	zh leisure
ē even	ur fur	ŋ ring
i hit		
ir here	ə = a *in* ago	
ī bite, fire	e *in* agent	
o lot	i *in* unity	
ō go	o *in* collect	
ô law, horn	u *in* focus	

Hamlet is a very old word that has gone through many changes. It is based on the Old English word for *home*.

Hurricane was an old Spanish word that meant "an evil spirit from the sea."

hygrometer

instructor

ivory

im·press (im pres′) *verb.* to affect strongly a person's ideas or feelings about someone or something: We were all *impressed* by his report. **impressed.**

in·de·pend·ence (in′di pen′dəns) *noun.* the condition of freedom from being controlled by others: The thirteen American colonies declared their *independence* from England in 1776.

in·flu·ence (in′floo wəns) *noun.* the power or ability to affect persons or things: He cannot *influence* me to do the wrong thing.

in·form (in fôrm′) *verb.* to tell about or give facts about something: She was *informed* that the train would arrive late. **informed.**

in·for·ma·tion (in′fər mā′shən) *noun.* **1.** something told; facts learned. **2.** something learned by reading, hearing, etc.

in·struct·or (in struk′tər) *noun.* a teacher or someone who teaches.

in·stru·ment (in′strə mənt) *noun.* **1.** a device used for making musical sounds: The piano is my favorite *instrument*. **2.** a tool used for a certain kind of work.

in·tel·li·gence (in tel′ə jəns) *noun.* the ability to learn, think, and understand.

in·ter·rupt (in tə rupt′) *verb.* **1.** to break into or upon something, such as someone talking; stop for awhile. **2.** to get in the way of; to cut off. **interrupted.**

i·vo·ry (ī′vər ē) *adjective.* **1.** made of the hard white substance that forms the tusks of elephants, walruses, etc.: *Ivory* is used to make piano keys. **2.** creamy-white in color.

J

jas·mine (jaz′min) *noun.* a tropical plant with fragrant white, red, or yellow flowers, one type of which is used to make perfume.

L

lane (lān) *noun.* **1.** a narrow path or road between hedges, walls, or buildings. **2.** a path for ships, cars, airplanes, etc., that are going in the same direction, as in a highway with four lanes. **lanes.**

leop·ard (lep′ərd) *noun.* a large, wild animal of the cat family, found in Africa and Asia. Leopards usually have a tan coat with black spots.

lev·ee (lev′ē) *noun.* **1.** a bank or pile of earth built along a river to keep it from overflowing: The people built *levees* to protect their homes from the flood. **2.** a place for ships to dock along a river. **levees.**

li·brar·i·an (lī brer′ē ən) *noun.* a person trained to work in a library.

loop (loop) *noun.* anything with a shape like a ring or a line that curves back to cross itself. **loops.**

lu·pine (loo′pin) *noun.* a garden plant with tall, white, pink, yellow, or blue flowers and pods with beanlike seeds. **lupines.**

M

meas·ure·ment (mezh′ər mənt) *noun.* the size, amount, etc., of something found by comparing it with something else: The carpenter carefully took the *measurement* of the boards with a ruler.

mel·o·dy (mel′ə dē) *noun.* musical tones arranged to make a tune or song, often the main part of a piece of music.

mem·o·ry (mem′ər ē) *noun.* **1.** the power of storing facts, ideas, names, etc., in the mind and recalling them as needed. **2.** all that can be remembered. **3.** a thought of someone or something from the past. **4.** the amount of information a computer can store or the parts of a computer that store information.

men·u (men′yoo) *noun.* **1.** the particular foods chosen for each course of a meal. **2.** a list of foods and drinks that can be ordered at a restaurant. **3.** a list of programs on a computer or a list of choices in a computer program.

a fat	oi oil	ch chin
ā ape	oo look	sh she
ä car, father	oo tool	th thin
e ten	ou out	*th* then
er care	u up	zh leisure
ē even	ur fur	ŋ ring
i hit		
ir here	ə = a *in* ago	
ī bite, fire	e *in* agent	
o lot	i *in* unity	
ō go	o *in* collect	
ô law, horn	u *in* focus	

———————◇———————

Leopard has two parts, *leo* and *pard*. *Leo* means "lion," and *pard* means "spotted animal."

lupine

mother-of-pearl

Nickname is a word that developed from a common mistake. The word *eke* used to mean "also" or "added." An *ekename* meant an "extra name." Over the years people began to say *nekename*. Finally, it changed to *nickname*.

noble

me·te·or·ol·o·gist (met'ē ə rol'ə jist) *noun.* a scientist who studies the weather, climate, and the earth's atmosphere.

mi·cro·scope (mī'krə skōp) *noun.* an instrument with a lens or group of lenses that makes tiny things look larger so that they can be seen easily.

mi·grate (mī'grāt) *verb.* **1.** to move from one country or place and settle in another. **2.** to move to a different place each season, as some animals do. **migrated.**

mi·nor (mi'nər) *adjective.* **1.** of lesser size, importance, amount, etc. **2.** in music, a tone that is one-half step from the next tone instead of one full step.

mois·ture (mois'chər) *noun.* water or other liquid that causes a slight wetness or dampness in the air.

moo (mо̄о̄) *verb.* to make the sound a cow makes. **mooed.**

moth·er·of·pearl (mu*th*'ər əv purl') *adjective.* made of the hard, pearly inside layer of certain seashells.

mourn (môrn) *verb.* to feel or show sorrow or grief over a loss, someone's death, etc. **mourned.**

N

nar·row (nar'ō) *adjective.* **1.** small in width as compared to length; not as wide as expected. **2.** small in size or amount.

nick·name (nik'nām) *noun.* name often used instead of the real name of a person, place, or thing, given in fun or out of strong liking: The tall boy's *nickname* is Stretch.

no·ble (nō'b'l) *noun.* a person who has a high rank or royal title. **nobles.**

nov·el (nov''l) *noun.* a long story, usually a book, about imaginary characters and events.

nu·mer·i·cal (nоо mer'i k'l *or* nyо̄о̄ mer'i k'l) *adjective.* **1.** shown as a number instead of a letter. **2.** of or having to do with a number or numbers.

O

ob·ject (ob′jikt) *noun.* a thing that can be seen or touched; something that has shape and takes up space. **objects.**

odds (odz) *plural noun.* a difference that makes one thing more likely to happen than another.

or·ches·tra (ôr′kis trə) *noun.* a group of people who play musical instruments together, usually in public.

or·di·nar·y (ôr′d′n er′ē) *adjective.* not special; normal; usual.

or·gan (ôr′gən) *noun.* **1.** a musical instrument with keys, pedals, and pipes of different sizes. Air is forced through the pipes to make different tones. **2.** a certain part of the body such as the heart or lungs.

ounce (ɵuns) *noun.* **1.** a small unit of weight equal to ¹/₁₆ of a pound. **2.** a measure of liquids—one fluid ounce is ¹/₁₆ of a pint. **3.** any small amount.

P

palm (päm) *noun.* any of a number of trees, found in warm parts of the world, with large leaves at the top of a tall, branchless trunk.

pas·ture (pas′chər) *verb.* **1.** to feed on growing grass. **2.** to put animals out to feed on growing grass: The farmer put the sheep out to *pasture* every day.

pa·tient (pā′shənt) *noun.* a person who is being treated by a doctor or dentist: Each of the *patients* waited her turn to see the doctor. **patients.** —*adjective.* able to put up with delays, pain, or troubles without complaining.

pat·tern (pat′ərn) *noun.* **1.** the way in which lines or the parts of something are put together; design or decoration such as a wallpaper pattern. **2.** a guide or model used when making things.

peas·ant (pez″nt) *noun.* a farm worker or farmer of a small farm in Europe. **peasants.**

a fat	ɵi oil	ch chin
ā ape	ᴔ look	sh she
ä car, father	ᴐᴐ tool	th thin
e ten	ou out	*th* then
er care	u up	zh leisure
ē even	ur fur	n̄g ring
i hit		
ir here	ə = a *in* ago	
ī bite, fire	e *in* agent	
o lot	i *in* unity	
ō go	o *in* collect	
ô law, horn	u *in* focus	

orchestra

organ pipes

357

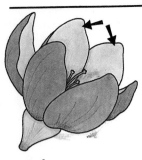

petals

possum

prow

per·suade (pər swād′) *verb.* to get someone to act or think a certain way by making it seem like a good idea. **persuaded.**

pet·al (pet″l) *noun.* one of the colorful leaves of a plant that forms the flower. **petals.**

phrase (frāz) *noun.* **1.** two or more words that give a single idea or mean something, but are not a complete sentence. **2.** a short passage of music, usually of two, four, or eight measures. **phrases.**

pierce (pirs) *verb.* **1.** to make a hole in. **2.** to go through or into. **pierced.**

plow·horse (plou′hôrs′) *noun.* a horse used to pull a farming tool that turns over the soil before seeds are planted. **plowhorses.**

pop·u·lar (pop′yə lər) *adjective.* **1.** liked by many people. **2.** very well liked by one's own friends. **3.** believed by many people, as in a popular idea.

po·si·tion (pə zish′ən) *noun.* **1.** the usual or proper way a person or thing is placed. **2.** the place where a person or thing is, especially how near or far from other things. **3.** a job that someone has. **positions.**

pos·sum (pos′əm) *noun. a shorter form of* **opossum.** a small American animal that lives in trees, carries its young in a pouch, and plays dead when it is in danger.

price (prīs) *noun.* the amount of money that is asked or given for something: The *price* of the dress I want to buy is $25.00.

prince (prins) *noun.* **1.** the son or grandson of a king, queen, or other royal ruler. **2.** a ruler whose rank is below that of a king.

pro·fes·sion·al (prə fesh′ən′l) *adjective.* **1.** of or about a person who earns a living at something that needs special learning or training: The tailor is proud of his *professional* skill. **2.** working in a particular job for pay, as a professional writer.

pro·test (prə test′) *verb.* to speak strongly against something; to disagree or object. **protested.**

prow (prou) *noun.* the front or forward part of a boat or ship. **prows.**

pu·pil (pyo͞o′p′l) *noun.* **1.** the round, dark opening in the center of the eye. **2.** a person, especially a young one, who is taught in a school or by a private teacher.

Q

quar·ter·size (kwôr′tər sīz′) *adjective.* equal to ¼ of the usual size.

R

ra·dar (rā′där) *noun.* a device that sends out and picks up radio waves that bounce off faraway objects. The radio waves are then used to locate objects.

ra·di·o·sonde (rā′dē ō sond′) *noun.* an instrument sent up by balloon and used to measure the temperature, humidity, and air pressure of the upper atmosphere.

re·al·ize (rē′ə līz) *verb.* **1.** to understand completely: I *realized* that my report would require a lot of time to prepare. **2.** to make real; bring into being; achieve. **realized.**

rec·i·pe (res′ə pē) *noun.* a list of ingredients and directions for making something to eat.

red·coat (red′kōt) *noun.* a British soldier at the time when they wore red coats,

as at the time of the American Revolution. **redcoats.**

re·flect (ri flekt′) *verb.* **1.** to give back an image, as a mirror or water does: The setting sun was *reflected* in the lake. **2.** to bend or throw back, as light, heat, sound, etc. **reflected.**

reg·i·ment (rej′ə mənt) *noun.* a group of soldiers who fight together as a unit.

re·hears·al (ri hur′səl) *noun.* time spent practicing in order to prepare for a performance.

rein (rān) *verb.* to guide, slow, or stop a horse by pulling long leather straps connected to each side of the metal bar in the horse's mouth. **reined.**

res·cue (res′kyōō) *verb.* to free or save from danger or harm: The lifeguard *rescued* the swimmer from drowning. **rescued.**

ret·i·na (ret″nə) *noun.* the lining at the back of the eyeball, which is sensitive to light. The image formed there is carried to the brain by the optic nerve.

rose-col·ored (rōz′kul′ərd) *adjective.* **1.** pinkish- or purplish-red in color. **2.** bright, cheerful, or hopeful.

a fat	oi oil	ch chin
ā ape	oo look	sh she
ä car, father	ōo tool	th thin
e ten	ou out	*th* then
er care	u up	zh leisure
ē even	ur fur	ng ring
i hit		
ir here	ə = a *in* ago	
ī bite, fire	e *in* agent	
o lot	i *in* unity	
ō go	o *in* collect	
ô law, horn	u *in* focus	

radar

Radar is made up of the first letters of the words in the phrase *Ra*dio *D*etecting *a*nd *R*anging, which is the longer name of the radar device.

RSVP has almost become a word in English, but it is not really a word. The letters are the first letters of four French words, *respondez s'il vous plait*. In French, the words mean "respond if you please." In modern English, RSVP is a polite way of asking someone to answer an invitation.

scroll

slope

rough (ruf) *adjective.* **1.** not smooth or level: The car rocked back and forth as it moved along the *rough* road. **2.** having bumps or projections; uneven. **3.** not gentle or careful.

roy·al (rɔi'əl) *adjective.* **1.** fit for a king or queen; magnificent; splendid. **2.** of, from, or by a king or queen. **3.** of a kingdom, its government, etc.

RSVP *or* **r.s.v.p.** *phrase.* initials of the French phrase meaning "please reply."

ru·in (rōo'in) *verb.* **1.** to damage or destroy. **2.** to make poor. **ruined.**

S

scan·ner (skan'ər) *noun.* a device that uses a beam of light to examine something.

scroll (skrōl) *noun.* **1.** a roll of paper or parchment with writing or pictures on it. **2.** a decoration in the form of a scroll.

scur·ry (skur'ē) *verb.* run quickly. **scurried.**

se·lec·tion (sə lek'shən) *noun.* **1.** a thing or things chosen.

2. a choosing or being chosen. **3.** things from which to choose.

shrug (shrug) *verb.* to draw the shoulders up toward the head to show that one does not care or does not know. **shrugged.**

sig·na·ture (sig'nə chər) *noun.* a person's name written in his or her own handwriting: Our teacher wrote her *signature* on the board.

skin·ner (skin'nər) *noun.* **1.** an old term for a person who steals or cheats. **2.** someone who strips animal skins or prepares them for sale. **skinners.**

slen·der (slen'dər) *adjective.* **1.** long and thin: James is *slender,* even though he eats a lot. **2.** small in size or amount.

slope (slōp) *noun.* **1.** land that is not flat; slanted like a hillside. **2.** a surface, line, etc., that slants.

sock·et (sok'it) *noun.* a hollow part into which something fits or which holds something: Carefully screw the light bulb into the *socket.*

so·lo·ist (sō′lō ist) *noun.* a performer who sings, dances, etc., alone on stage, or a person who does something alone.

sound spec·to·graph (sound′ spek′tə graf) *noun.* a machine that makes pictures from sounds that people make when they speak.

splot (splot) *noun. shortened form of* **splotch.** an uneven spot, splash, or stain.

stamp (stamp) *verb.* **1.** to bring or put the foot down hard. **2.** to put a postage stamp on a letter or package to be mailed.

stand·ard (stan′dərd) *adjective.* **1.** of or about anything used and accepted as the rule or model. **2.** not special or extra; ordinary.

steam sho·vel (stēm′ shuv″l) *noun.* a large, mechanically operated digger powered by steam. **steam shovels.**

ster·ling sil·ver (stur′ling sil′vər) *noun.* silver that is at least 92.5% pure, often used to make coins or jewelry.

stur·dy (stur dē) *adjective.* strongly built; made to last a long time.

sub·way (sub′wā) *noun.* an underground railroad on which people travel from one place to another in some large cities.

swirl (swurl) *adjective.* to move by twisting or spinning around and around: The strong wind blew *swirling* snow over the fields. **swirling.**

a fat	**oi** oil	**ch** chin
ā ape	**oo** look	**sh** she
ä car, father	**ōō** tool	**th** thin
e ten	**ou** out	***th*** then
er care	**u** up	**zh** leisure
ē even	**ur** fur	**ng** ring
i hit		
ir here	**ə** = a *in* ago	
ī bite, fire	e *in* agent	
o lot	i *in* unity	
ō go	o *in* collect	
ô law, horn	u *in* focus	

T

tech·nol·o·gy (tek nol′ə jē) *noun.* the use of scientific ideas to invent tools to solve everyday problems.

tem·per·a·ture (tem′prə chər *or* tem pər′ə chər) *noun.* **1.** the degree of heat or cold: The *temperature* today is too cool for us to go to the beach. **2.** a human body heat above the normal 98.6 degrees.

ther·mom·e·ter (thər mom′ə tər) *noun.* a device that measures temperature.

thong (thông) *noun.* a narrow strip of leather used as a lace, strap, etc.

thorn (thôrn) *noun.* a short, sharp point that grows on the stems of some plants such as rose bushes: Be careful not to prick your finger on the *thorns.* **thorns.**

thermometer

rose **thorns**

361

tor·na·do (tôr nā'dō) *noun.* a tall, thin column of air that whirls very fast and moves along, destroying things in its path. **tornados** or **tornadoes.**

treas·ure (trezh'ər) *noun.* **1.** a collection of valuable things such as money, gold, etc. **2.** a person or thing that is greatly loved.

tre·men·dous (tri men'dəs) *adjective.* **1.** very large or huge. **2.** wonderful; marvelous.

trom·bone (trom bōn' *or* trom'bōn) *noun.* a brass musical instrument with a long, bent tube that slides in and out to change the sounds it makes.

trop·i·cal (trop'i k'l) *adjective.* of, in, or about the very hot climates of the earth, near the equator.

trudge (truj) *verb.* to walk slowly, as if very tired: We saw John *trudging* up the hill after he jogged two miles. **trudging.**

trum·pet (trum'pit) *noun.* a brass instrument with a long, looped tube that ends in a funnellike opening.

type (tīp) *verb.* to write with a typewriter; to use such a machine to produce printed words.

violin

U

u·nit (yoo'nit) *noun.* **1.** a fixed amount used to measure. **2.** a single thing, person, or object that is part of a larger group. **units.**

un·u·su·al (un yoo'zhoo wəl) *adjective.* not common, usual, or ordinary; rare: It's *unusual* to have such warm weather in February.

V

val·u·a·ble (val'yoo b'l *or* val'yoo wə b'l) *adjective.* **1.** worth a lot of money. **2.** thought of as important or very useful.

ver·sion (vur'zhən) *noun.* a story told from one point of view; a different form of something: People who saw the accident told the police different *versions* of who caused it. **versions.**

vi·o·la (vē ō'lə) *noun.* a stringed musical instrument that is like a violin, but larger and with a deeper tone.

vi·o·lin (vī ə lin') *noun.* a musical instrument with four strings, played with a bow.

vi·o·lin·ist (vī ə lin′ist) *noun.* a person who plays the violin.

vol·un·teer (vol′ən tir′) *verb.* to do something out of choice, of one's own free will. **volunteered.**

W

wharf (hwôrf) *noun.* a long platform built from the shore out over the water, so that ships can easily discharge passengers and unload cargo. **wharves.**

whirl·ing (hwurl′iñg) *adjective.* quickly spinning around and around.

whoosh (hwo͞osh *or* wo͞osh) *verb.* to move with a loud hissing sound. **whooshed.**

winch (winch) *noun.* a machine that uses a chain or rope to pull or lift things.

wis·dom (wiz′dəm) *noun.* the quality of intelligence and good judgment that tells one what to do and what is right or wrong.

work·shop (wurk′shäp) *noun.* **1.** a place where work is done. **2.** a meeting where a group of people study, talk, or work on special projects: Our teacher went to three *workshops* to learn about new ways to use classroom materials. **workshops.**

X

x-ray (eks′rā′) *noun.* an invisible ray used to take pictures of an object or the inside of the body: On my first visit, the dentist took *x-rays* of my teeth to check for cavities. **x-rays.**

a fat	oi oil	ch chin
ā ape	o͝o look	sh she
ä car, father	o͞o tool	th thin
e ten	ou out	*th* then
er care	u up	zh leisure
ē even	ur fur	ñg ring
i hit		
ir here	ə = a *in* ago	
ī bite, fire	e *in* agent	
o lot	i *in* unity	
ō go	o *in* collect	
ô law, horn	u *in* focus	

wharf

X-rays were named by the man who discovered them in 1895. He called them x-rays because, at first, he didn't know what they were. The practice of labeling something unknown with an *x* goes back to the Middle Ages.

ABOUT THE AUTHORS

The authors listed below have written some of the selections that appear in this book. The content of the notes was determined by a survey of what readers wanted to know about authors.

VERNA AARDEMA

VERNA AARDEMA

Verna Aardema's last name is pronounced ar′də mə. She began writing stories because her little girl liked to listen to a story while she was eating. "She could make a scrambled egg last all the way through 'Little Red Riding Hood,' so I began to make up little feeding stories. That way she didn't know how far off the end would be." Later, Verna Aardema began writing and publishing the stories she told to her daughter. *(Born 1911)*

GARY APPLE

Gary Apple lives in New York City. He writes plays, funny stories, and scripts for television. He believes that young writers should not be afraid to put their ideas on paper. He says, "If you think of a poem or a story or a play or just an idea you like, write it down. Don't worry if it's good or bad, just put it on paper. You can go back later and change what you have written, but first you have to have the ideas on paper. Your creative thoughts are wonderful things. Writing is a way to save those thoughts forever."

GARY APPLE

GWENDOLYN BROOKS

The poet Gwendolyn Brooks was born in Topeka, Kansas. She says, "I loved poetry very early and began to put rhymes together at about seven. At the age of thirteen my poem 'Eventide' was accepted and printed in a children's magazine." When she was sixteen she began submitting poems to a newspaper, and more than 75 of them were published. Gwendolyn Brooks won the Pulitzer Prize in poetry in 1950 for "Annie Allen." *(Born 1917)*

GWENDOLYN BROOKS

DROLLENE P. BROWN

Drollene P. Brown grew up in West Virginia and now lives in Florida. Before writing her first book, she worked at several different jobs. Her book *Sybil Rides for Independence* is about a real person who lived more than 200 years ago. Ms. Brown also wrote another book about a real person who lived about 100 years ago. That book told the story of Belva Lockwood, a woman who ran for president in 1884. Ms. Brown enjoys writing about interesting people who lived long ago. She also enjoys meeting young readers and talking to them. *(Born 1940)*

CARL CARMER

CARL CARMER

Many of the books Carl Carmer wrote were illustrated by his wife, Elizabeth Black Carmer. He and his wife also wrote some books together. Carl Carmer said that as a child, he was "fascinated by the sound and color of words." He thought that books for young people should be simple but well-written. "I take my writings for kids just as seriously as for adults." *(1893–1976)*

ELIZABETH CARMER

Elizabeth Carmer grew up in New Orleans. She says she enjoyed drawing from the time she was a little girl. "With the first crayons and chalks came the desire to paint." After she married Carl Carmer, she moved to New York. She and her husband wrote books together. She also illustrated some of the books he wrote. *(Born 1904)*

MARY BLOUNT CHRISTIAN

Mary Blount Christian was born in Houston, Texas. She is married and has three children. All her life she has been interested in writing. She says: "As an only child, I told stories to myself and my imaginary playmates, rewrote fairy tales into plays to present to the neighborhood children, and wrote stories (mostly scary ones) on scraps of paper." She has written a number of books and is working on writing more. *(Born 1933)*

MARY BLOUNT CHRISTIAN

MARCHETTE CHUTE

MARCHETTE CHUTE

Marchette Chute writes both poetry and nonfiction books. Many of her books are written because she gets curious about something. She says, "I set out to find everything I can about it." She enjoys looking things up, even when the research takes a long time. "The research and the writing," she says, "is sometimes very slow, but I never fail to enjoy myself, just as I never fail to start my next book with the same sense of delighted curiosity about what I will find." Marchette Chute lives in New York City. She does most of her research at the New York Public Library. *(Born 1909)*

BEVERLY CLEARY

BEVERLY CLEARY

Beverly Cleary says that she had a hard time learning to read when she was young. After she learned to read, she wondered why there weren't books about "plain ordinary boys and girls. Why couldn't authors write about the sort of boys and girls who lived on my block?" She decided that when she grew up she would write books about ordinary people. Beverly Cleary has won many awards for her books, including the Newbery Medal. *(Born 1916)*

VICKI COBB

Vicki Cobb was born in New York City. She has written many nonfiction books for young people. Before she began writing books, she was a high school science teacher. She says that she tries to make science interesting for people who think it's a dull or difficult subject. *(Born 1938)*

VICKI COBB

BARBARA COONEY

Barbara Cooney writes and illustrates her books for young people. She also illustrates books by other authors. She won the Caldecott Medal for *Chanticleer and the Fox*. This story was first told by Geoffrey Chaucer, an English poet who lived in the 1300s. Barbara Cooney retold Chaucer's story and illustrated it with beautiful drawings. *(Born 1917)*

BARBARA COONEY

LINDA GOSS

LINDA GOSS

Linda Goss loves to tell stories. Some of the stories she tells are new stories. Some of them are old. She tells stories she has heard from other people, and she makes up her own stories, too. When Linda Goss tells stories, she doesn't use just her voice. She also uses her hands, her face, pieces of cloth, and jewelry. Before she starts a story, she rings bells to tell people to gather around her because the story is about to begin. Linda Goss is the "Official Storyteller of Philadelphia."

GAIL E. HALEY

GAIL E. HALEY

Gail E. Haley writes and illustrates books for young people. She has won many awards, including the Kate Greenaway Medal and the Ralph Caldecott Medal. She says many people ask her what it's like to be a Caldecott winner. "They might as well ask: 'What is it like to become Miss America, a Nobel Laureate, or a winner of the Irish Sweepstakes?' Any of these are wildly happy surprises—frosting on the cake of life." *(Born 1939)*

MARGARET HILLERT

Margaret Hillert writes poems and stories. She also teaches school. "In my poetry and stories," she says, "I write about things I like myself: *cats*, Teddy bears, biking, *cats,* colored leaves, *cats,* etc. One of my cats usually sits on my chest and 'helps' — or sits on my lap at the typewriter." Margaret Hillert has been writing poems since she was in the third grade. *(Born 1920)*

EFNER TUDOR HOLMES

Efner Tudor Holmes was born in Boston, Massachusetts. She is married and has two children. She says that she writes about animals and country living because she likes both these things. She is also interested in farming, music, and travel. Her mother, Tasha Tudor, is a well-known illustrator of children's books. *(Born 1949)*

Lee Bennett Hopkins

LEE BENNETT HOPKINS

Lee Bennett Hopkins has interviewed, or talked with, many writers and illustrators. He writes about his talks with these people. He also writes poems for young people. He says, "I love doing children's books. Each one is a new challenge, a new day, a new spring for me." Lee Bennett Hopkins also puts together anthologies, or collections, of other people's poems. He goes through thousands of poems and chooses the twenty that he thinks children will enjoy most. *(Born 1938)*

Langston Hughes

LANGSTON HUGHES

Langston Hughes said he began to write poetry because he was elected Class Poet when he was in grammar school. He said, "The day I was elected, I went home and wondered what I should write. Since we had eight teachers in our school, I thought there should be one verse for each teacher, with an especially good one for my favorite teacher." When he grew up, he wrote many poems. He also wrote stories and novels. Langston Hughes won many awards for his writing. *(1902–1967)*

JOHANNA HURWITZ

Johanna Hurwitz is a writer and illustrator of books for young people. She is also a children's librarian. She says, "My parents met in a bookstore, and there has never been a moment when books were not important in my life. I loved the library so much that I made the firm decision by age ten that someday I would become a librarian." At the same time, she planned that she would write books, too. Johanna Hurwitz says she writes many letters to friends and relatives. "I am sure the letter writing that I do has been the best type of training for my writing books." *(Born 1937)*

JOHANNA HURWITZ

JEANETTE LEARDI

Jeanette Leardi lives in New York City. She is a writer and an editor. She writes articles for *Child Life* and *Sesame Street Magazine* and also writes poetry. She wanted to be a writer since she was in the sixth grade, when she helped to start a school newspaper. She says, "I believe that there are two things that anyone who wants to be a writer must do: read a lot and write a lot." She also believes that it is important to write about something you care about, and adds, "Don't get discouraged if you don't write exactly what you want to say. With practice all writers become better writers." *(Born 1952)*

JEANETTE LEARDI

ARNOLD LOBEL

ARNOLD LOBEL

Arnold Lobel wrote and illustrated books for children. Many of his books have won awards. *Frog and Toad Are Friends* was a Caldecott Honor Book, and *Frog and Toad Together* was a Newbery Honor Book. Arnold Lobel enjoyed creating books for children. He once said, "There is a little world at the end of my pencil. I am the stage director, the costume designer, and the man who pulls the curtain. When a character is not behaving as I would wish him to, he can be quickly dismissed with a wave of my eraser." *(1933–1987)*

MISKA MILES

MISKA MILES

Miska Miles's real name was Patricia Miles Martin. She wrote many stories and poems for children. Several of her books were Junior Literary Guild selections and American Library Association Notable Books. She said she began writing when she was a young child visiting her grandfather's farm in Kansas. "At Grandfather's, I used to go up into the barn loft. The barn was always partly full of hay, and the smell was dusty and sweet. I remember sitting in the big open doorway listening to the rain on the roof, smelling the sweet country fragrance, a lined tablet on my lap, describing the things I saw and smelled and heard." *(1899–1986)*

MOTHER GOOSE

Mother Goose may or may not have been a real person. Some people say she was. Some people say she was not. The name *Mother Goose* was first used in France more than three hundred years ago. In the early 1700s, in Boston, there was a woman named Elizabeth Goose. She sang rhymes to her seven small grandchildren. The children's father is said to have collected the rhymes and verses, but the book has never been found. Even if that woman was Mother Goose, she did not make up the rhymes she sang. Many of them are known to be three or four hundred years old. A few of them are said to be even older.

MOTHER GOOSE

EVALINE NESS

Evaline Ness wrote books for children. She also illustrated her own books and the books of other authors. She said that it was hard to illustrate her own books. She thought that her books should be published with blank spaces for readers to draw their own pictures. The publishers did not agree with her. She won many awards, including the Caldecott Medal for *Sam, Bangs & Moonshine*. Several of her books were also Caldecott Honor Books and American Library Association Notable Books. *(1911–1986)*

EVALINE NESS

MICHELLE NIKLY

Michelle Nikly lives in Europe. When she wrote *The Emperor's Plum Tree,* she wrote it in French. The story was published in France. Then someone decided that it would be a good story for children in the United States to read. So the story was retold in English.

DANIEL MANUS PINKWATER

DANIEL MANUS PINKWATER

Daniel Manus Pinkwater writes and illustrates books for young people. He enjoyed reading when he was growing up. He says Mark Twain is his favorite author. After he graduated from college, he worked for several years as a sculptor. When Daniel Manus Pinkwater began writing books, he was more interested in the illustrations than the writing. He says, "Writing was a bit of a challenge. Then the stories became more interesting to me." Some of Daniel Manus Pinkwater's books have been American Library Association Notable Books and Junior Literary Guild selections. *(Born 1941)*

CHARLES M. SCHULZ

CHARLES M. SCHULZ

Charles M. Schulz is the man who created the comic strip *Peanuts.* He says that Snoopy, the dog in *Peanuts,* was modeled after a dog he had when he was growing up. His dog was called Spike. Charles Schulz says, "I had decided that the dog in the strip was to be named 'Sniffy,' until one day, just before the strip was actually to be published, I was walking past a newsstand and glanced down the rows of comic magazines. There I saw one about a dog named Sniffy, so I had to think of another name. Fortunately, before I even got home, I recalled my mother once saying that if we ever had another dog, we should name him 'Snoopy.' " That is how Snoopy got his name. *(Born 1922)*

ELIZABETH SHUB

ELIZABETH SHUB

Elizabeth Shub was born in Poland. She came to the United States when she was a child. She writes books for children, and she won the American Library Association award for her book, *The White Stallion.* She also translates books into English for other writers. She helped Isaac Bashevis Singer translate *Zlateh the Goat, and Other Stories* from Yiddish.

WILLIAM STEIG

WILLIAM STEIG

William Steig writes and illustrates books for young people. He did not begin writing for children until he was nearly seventy years old. Before that, he drew cartoons for magazines. Now, he has won many awards for his books for young people. Two of his most important awards are the Newbery Medal and the Caldecott Medal. He once said, "Winning is definitely fun. I never understood what was missing from my life until this began to happen. It feels darn good." *(Born 1907)*

CHRIS VAN ALLSBURG

CHRIS VAN ALLSBURG

Chris Van Allsburg is an author and illustrator. He has won many awards for his work. He received the Caldecott Medal for *Jumanjii.* Some of his other books have been Caldecott Honor Books, American Library Association Notable Books, and Boston Globe–Horn Book honor books. He began creating children's books when his wife started teaching school. She would bring books home from school and tell him that he, too, could write good books. Chris Van Allsburg says he enjoys getting letters from people who have read his books. *(Born 1949)*

DIANE WOLKSTEIN

Diane Wolkstein lives in New York City. She is a writer of children's books. Some of her books have been chosen as American Library Association Notable Books. Diane Wolkstein is also a storyteller. She teaches storytelling to teachers and librarians. She has made records of stories from different lands and has traveled to Europe to tell her stories. *(Born 1942)*

DIANE WOLKSTEIN

ED YOUNG

Ed Young was born in Tientsin, China, the son of Qua-Ling and Yuen Teng Young. He attended City College of San Francisco and the University of Illinois and did graduate study at Pratt Institute. He is the illustrator of a number of books. Ed Young has received many awards. He received the Caldecott runner-up award for his illustrations of *The Emperor and the Kite;* the Horn Book Honor List and Child Study Association Book Award for *Chinese Mother Goose Rhymes. The Girl Who Loved the Wind* was named a Children's Book Showcase title. Ed Young also teaches a Chinese exercise called Tai Chi Chuan, which he learned from an old Chinese master. He says he "finds Tai Chi Chuan beneficial to both mind and body; the whole of the person. This exercise has had profound influence upon my way of thinking and on the things I do." *(Born 1931)*

ED YOUNG

AUTHOR INDEX

1981 by Harper & Row, (b) from *Annie and the Old One* by Miska Miles, illustrated by Peter Parnall, published in 1971 by Little, Brown; 258, *Umbrellas in the Rain,* 1899, Maurice Prendergast, American, 1859–1924, Watercolor, 13 5/8″ × 20 1/2″, Charles Henry Hayden Fund, Museum of Fine Arts, Boston; 270–278, Glenn Oakley; 280, (b) Stephanie Maze/Woodfin Camp, Inc., © 1985 National Geographic Society; 281, (tl) map division: The New York Public Library, Astor, Lenox, and Tilden Foundations, (tr) David R. Austin/ Stock Boston, (b) Jeffrey Cardenas/*Time Magazine*; 317, (tl) reproduced with permission of Atheneum Publishers, an imprint of Macmillan Publishing Company from *Cloudy with a Chance of Meatballs* by Judi Barrett, illustrated by Ron Barrett, drawings copyright © 1978 Ron Barrett, (tr) from *From the Hills of Georgia: An Autobiography in Paintings* by Mattie Lou O'Kelley, published in 1983 by Little, Brown, (bl) from *Island Winter* by Charles Martin, published in 1986 by Greenwillow, (br) from *First Snow* by Helen Coutant, pictures by V-Dinh; 346, Ruth Lacey; 349, Ruth Lacey; 350, Stephen G. Maka; 351, Ruth Lacey; 352, © Frank Siteman 1988; 354, Richard Pasley/Stock Boston, Ira Kirschenbaum/Stock Boston; 355, Tom Pantages; 356, © Frank Siteman 1988, Bettmann Archive; 357, Milton Feinberg/Stock Boston, Gregg Mancuso/Stock Boston; 358, L. West/Bruce Coleman, Inc.; 359, Tom Pantages; 361, © Frank Siteman 1988; 363, Gale Zucker/Stock Boston; 364, 365, (b) *Los Angeles Times*; 367, Macmillian Publishing Company; 368, (t) Bettmann Archive; 369, (b) Viking Penguin; 370, (t) Ken Kauffman; 372, (t) provided by author; 373, Viking Penguin; 374, (b) Little, Brown and Company; 375, (t) Bettmann Archive, (b) H.W. Wilson Company; 376, V. Bella-Smith; 377, (t) Viking Penguin, (b) H.W. Wilson Company; 378, (t) Nancy Crampton, (b) Houghton Mifflin Company; 379, (t) H.W. Wilson Company.

G H I J—VHP—96 95 94 93 92 91 90 89